No E

James Rose

Copyright © 2022 James Rose

All rights reserved.

ISBN: 9798532666382

Foreword

Before agreeing to help write this book I had never even met James.

What an incredible man !

He has achieved some amazing things, despite his disabilities. I found this experience both informative and fascinating. Before losing his legs, James was a soldier And this book is written in typical Army Jargon I have really enjoyed working with James, it has been an eye opener. I look forward to his future adventures with great interest, because I am sure that
they will also be epic. His book is an easy read, but very compelling too.
I hope that you enjoy it as much as I have..

Geoff Mitchell
International Athletics Coach

Contents

1. The Lad I used to be
2. Afghanistan or bust
3. Big mistake
4. The darkest of days
5. A light at the end of the tunnel
6. The biggest challenge of my life
7. it's a funny ol' life
8. Invictus Becons
9. Climb every mountain
10. No turning back

Acknowldgements

CHAPTER ONE

THE LAD I USED TO BE

Hi, my name is James Rose and this book is my story.

Born in the North East of England, a place called Middlesbrough which, like any large town or city, has its bad parts, although the media always seem to concentrate on these when they broadcast their 'revelations'.

Yes, we have high unemployment, but that's hardly our fault. When the Government decided to close the coal mines in our area in the 1980s it had a knock-on effect, Dockers were laid off because we weren't exporting as much coal as before, the steelworks closed because the fuel they needed for the furnaces now had to be

expensively imported from Chile, and the chemical works (ICI) also became too
expensive to run.

The industrial heart was knocked out of our town, what they left us with was decaying, rusting old sites that nobody wants to move into. Nowadays we import the coal and the steel that these men used to provide, and many of these proud men have been forced into a life on benefits.

People who come from this area get the nickname 'Smoggies' because of the large cloud of smoke that used to hang over the town: it's no longer there- but neither are the jobs! The nickname, though, endures. Where I live is beautiful; modern housing nestled on the edge of the countryside.

The explorer Captain James Cook was born very close to here and we are only about 5 miles from the northern slopes of the North Yorkshire Moors, with its sleepy little villages and patchwork quilt of dry-stone framed fields. Whitby, Robin Hood's Bay, Redcar and Saltburn are all very close, on the coast, just to the south. Who would want to live anywhere else?Certainly a complete contrast to the hot, sweaty, dusty region that I found myself in later on in my chosen career.

Growing up in Cleveland I had a pretty normal childhood really. Playing out and causing mischief with my friends, but my favourite thing to do was to play FOOTBALL - I felt I was born to play it!

Right from primary school I made my mark as a left winger and regular scorer for my school team. When I went to secondary school I improved even more, I made the school team where my development accelerated. I thrived, playing not only for the school, but also for the Junior teams at our local Club; Tontine Juniors.

I loved it! I couldn't imagine life without it! It was all I ever wanted to do - every weekend was crammed with football. Saturdays were our training days and Sunday was match day.

Now when I say I loved it, not EVERY aspect of the game was enjoyable though! I will never forget how cold some mornings were. We would warm up thoroughly and extensively, but the cold seemed to permeate right to the core of our bodies. Every time I kicked the ball it would be like kicking a block of ice.

I would wear thermals, a hat and fingerless gloves and yet still I felt like a snowman!
We won many games throughout my junior career, but one of the highlights had to be when we were invited to an international tournament in Holland. We played against numerous 'class' teams from different countries, it was an experience I'll never forget.

We reached the semi-finals and were beaten 1-0. BUT, even though beaten, I was so happy to hear the final whistle. I was absolutely exhausted; their winger was like shit off a stick - really, really quick - and I had to track him back every time he moved. I
did my job well, I never stopped running and tackling. He was as good as I'd ever played - the final whistle and the hot shower afterwards came as a blessed relief.
As I grew older, unfortunately as with so many other teenagers, those days were left behind - I discovered GIRLS, and drinking, and the wrong crowd to hang out with.

Leaving School & starting a career were far in the long distant future, I never really bothered considering what I would do when I left. No plan - No career path.
So, when the end of schooldays came, it was a shock! I basically fell into the first job that came along and became a kitchen porter. I knew then, though, that this wasn't the job I wanted to do for the rest of my life, it was only temporary while
I sorted my life out! Suddenly, like a thunderbolt, it hit me! - Join the Army, that's what I'll do, join the bloody Army! I rang the Army Recruiting Office.

It seemed like an eternity before I was given my interview; but how relieved was I when I passed. That was in 2005. Later that year I went to the AFCH (Army Foundation College) in Harrogate. This 'career move'

lasted a whole 5 months before I realised that, in truth, this really wasn't for
me!

I remember arriving back home and my Mam was soooo disappointed that I had packed it in. I felt I had let her down, so I promised myself and my Mam that I would join up again when I was a bit older.
I loved army life and I knew it was what I wanted to do, but I guess that, at such a young age, I was just too immature to appreciate that!
Fast forward 3 years and I re-enlisted. This time, being older, I knew I couldn't leave for at least 5 years, BUT this time I was ready! And now I couldn't wait to get started!

My initial training, this time around, was at Catterick, where I underwent six solid months of gruelling (and I mean gruelling) infantry training. I embraced it and really got stuck in, whilst inwardly wishing that I'd continued with my football training and not discovered the booze. I was really unfit and struggling!
At first I found it so hard, I realised that I was totally out of condition. It didn't occur to me that everybody else was having the same problems. It wasn't until we came back after our first leave and we repeated the 1.5 mile run test (that was our gauge to our fitness), that the penny dropped. I came second in the whole platoon!!! This delighted me. I was close to the back the first time we completed this test but this time . . . !

The dreaded gas chamber drill was fast approaching I had heard bad things about this place as we waited outside with full NBC kit on and already wearing our gas masks. We were ordered in one by one and told to start walking around in a circle then you would be grabbed into the middle and told to take your gas mask off and shout GAS GAS GAS, while trying not inhale any gas but it was just to bad, as soon as you inhaled any you would burst into fits of coughing choking which put you in a state of panic.

After 2-3 minutes you were kicked out to recover!! worse 3 minute of my life!!!

My 6 month's of training was coming to an end now and I couldnt wait to parade in front of my family I was really proud of myself and loved every minute of training now it was time to join my battalion!

August 2008 and my time had come to move to blackpool were my regiment was based 10 minute taxi ride from Blackpool.

I will never forget my first day I turned up and realised I had forgot my beret and never had a room to sleep in after arriving at camp at 0100 in the morning. Good job my brother was in the same regiment as me as he had a spare beret and let me sleep on his floor in his room "not the best start to battalion life"

Parade was at 0800 that was the day I found out I was heading straight to the Falklands on a 7 week exercise I couldn't wait to get stuck in.

We arrived at the falklands after an 18 hour flight with 1 stop over my first impression was "where the hell am I" there was nothing there apart from open ground and a massive base were most of the military personal on the island were accommodated in here it was huge.

Luckily enough my brother was allocating everyone rooms and he pushed me into a room he thought I would be ok as I was newbie or as there say in the Army RED ASS. 4 men to every room and I was the freshest in there so as you can imagine I was pretty shy and quite but that soon changed when we all got pissed and broke the Ice it turned out we had a lot in common after all!!

I think out of the 7 weeks we were there we were pissed for 5 of them although we got put on a drinking ban we still had our sources of finding the old devil juice but keeping it quiet was the hardest especially when our Platoon sergeant (Wrighty) would come in our room on the morning and it would smell like a brewery, he knew what we were upto hahahahah

Turns out the lads who was in that room with me are 2 of my closest mates still to this day.

I didn't HAVE to go to Afghanistan but, in September 2009, I volunteered!

I embarked on my first operational tour there . . . in the Gareshk Upper Valley, Helmand Province.

I always remember not being on the deployment list to go on tour and being VERY disappointed; I wanted to go, so, I asked to go!

My wish was granted, and I felt real pride and honour relaying this good news to my friends and family. I felt on top of the world.

When the day finally arrived to say goodbye to everyone; not for good - just for 6 months. It was the hardest goodbye of my life, not knowing deep down what I was going into and if I would return in one piece (or not at all!)

Suddenly, I felt really vulnerable and pretty fucking scared if I am being honest.

My major regret in signing up for this jaunt was leaving my girlfriend Naiomi (who would become my wife in the future)! We only met about a year earlier, and it was hard! Also leaving my family behind and my son Jake. Who was way to young to even understand what I was going into, we played call of duty a lot so I would try and explain to him that this is what I will be doing but he was to caught up in the computer he game he never took any notice.

I promised to write to her and phone her regularly. As I walked away, I assured her that it would soon all be over and I would be back before she knew it

. . . little did I know . . .

CHAPTER TWO

AFGHANISTAN OR BUST

I knew Afghanistan was going to be HOT, but nothing could prepare me for just HOW HOT! In total contrast, Brize Norton, in Oxfordshire, was grey and austere on that bleak September morning and I couldn't wait to board my first class (ha, ha!) RAF flight to Afghanistan.

In true RAF style, everything went like clockwork. It was a long flight and, like many of my 'experienced' colleagues on board, I should have got some sleep. But I was too excited! Fortunately, though, the journey was broken up with a stop in Dubai, where we picked up our connecting flight to Kandahar.

I felt a real surge of adrenaline as we boarded the next plane. This was a REAL military plane - the last one was like an RAF adapted tourist plane, the sort you'd take on your summer holidays to Greece, but this one was a big ass military plane to say the least - an C-17, I think - and it was pretty damn awesome.

Now this flight was much shorter, it seemed that we had no sooner found our seats and packed our kit away that an announcement was made over the tannoy - "Attention, please put on your body armour and helmets and prepare to land."

The lights went out and we began our decent into Kandahar. This was it . . . no turning back now! The realisation of where I was nervously sank in!

The back of Big Ass opened up and the ramp SLAMMED into the tarmac.

Then the heat and the dust slapped me in the face like a big, hot, sweaty blanket.

SHIT ! ! ! - THIS WAS IT!!!

When we arrived at Camp we were shown our temporary accommodation. It was BASIC, just a tent with beds in, washrooms and toilets - but what more did we need? We wouldn't be staying long.

We were given a fortnight to acclimatise to the extreme weather conditions before going out on patrol. This two-week period was not wasted, however, we spent it going to briefings about the area, the enemy, and other essential information intended to keep us alive - so obviously, we listened intently.

And, of course, very importantly, in our spare time, we topped up our suntans.

A lot of first-hand info was also picked up from our colleagues; men who had just returned from the front, telling us about their experiences

I was shitting myself, but at the same time I was pumped up and eager to get out there and earn my pay.

One last talk with the padre, a check that all of my kit was in full working order, one last call home, and then we boarded the chopper to be flown out into the dark unknown!

Unfortunately, numerous flight delays saw me reading through a multitude of newspapers and magazines, - in each one ALWAYS checking my horoscope to foretell what the coming days and weeks had in store for me!?!

Eventually, it arrived! The chopper that was to transfer us closer to the front line touched down. It flew us to a place called Gareshk!

I sat in the chopper like Rambo; flying 100 feet above the ground looking out onto the dark desert ground with my weapon, an LMG, in my arms.

The LMG is a LIGHT MACHINE GUN; I was also carrying 1000 plus rounds of ammunition, grenades and water.

As we got closer, you could hear activity on the ground - mainly loud bangs or flares going off in the night sky, these were intended to light up the enemy so that they could be taken out. My adrenaline was REALLY pumping now, and I thought my heart was busting through my chest!

We landed into FOB Keenan, and it was pitch black.

It was different to how I thought it would be. It was busy with British, Danish and other NATO forces scurrying about. Incredibly, there was also a shop selling all the home comforts - pop, sweets, crisps, chocolate, - all the good stuff! There were two computers, and most importantly, a phone to call your loved ones back at home!

Our mobile phones had been taken from us, to prevent us been compromised!

I felt like I was in a movie!

Our accommodation was nothing short of basic, eight or so beds with nets over to keep the nasties out! Amazingly, we had a PlayStation in there too! (Morale booster).

I picked mine, dropped my kit, and began to take in my surroundings.

Not impressed!!!

However, I was so tired out, and not caring, it took me only seconds to fall into a deep slumber, I can't remember my head hitting the pillow.

Wakeup call was at 0600hrs, shit shower shave (SS&S), and then breakfast with the team.

Familiarisation of the camp began. Numerous briefs on the area, the locals and much more important information . . . Finally, we were told that our first patrol would be the next morning at 0800 hours.

I didn't sleep that night ,,. all my nerves and scared feelings had vanished, I was alive and awake.

I was hungry; I was doing the soldiering thing that I'd signed up for. This was happening NOW, and I was here.

So, with my LMG and a pack full of grenades and ammunition, nobody was getting in my way. I felt prepared. All my endless training and briefings were coming together. Everything was kicking in.

Everything I had ever done in training was for this moment.

My role was part of the OMLT (Operating Mentor Liaison Team) - we would be mentoring the ANA

(Afghan National Army). Easy Peasy; or so it sounded, but it was fucking hard work to say the least.

Our first patrol would see us out on the front line of the most dangerous place on earth for three sweltering hours in 50 degrees of heat, with 70lbs on my back plus my weapon system which was heavy and bulky. my kit weighed more than me! I was only just 10 stone, and this kit felt like I had a house on my back. I remember taking a knee when my platoon commander spoke to one of the locals, my kit was so heavy on my back that when it came to standing back up again I staggered and struggled, and took ages. Lord knows what the old gent thought of this kid that they'd sent into battle to protect them all!

I couldn't wait to get back to camp to take this elephant off my back.

When we did finally arrive back, it was to the usual, monotonous but very necessary routine: unload our weapons at the front gate, head back to our room for a debriefing and then refuel in the scoff house. Then we could relax in the FOB.

Most of the boys would strip off and sunbathe... I loved to sunbathe! We'd been hardly any time at all in Afghanistan before I became so tanned that I could pass off for a local farmer - which could have its uses at a later date!

This relaxation time, however, was also when the pranksters were rife!

The showers were always a great setting for these . . . The showers were only about one minute's walk from our bunks, but to get there we had to walk round the other side of the camp.

We kept our fingers crossed, hoping that there wasn't a queue, otherwise all the hot water would be used up and it would be cold shower time.

Waiting for the lads to shower so we could pinch their towels and clothes, we would do anything to keep us amused and keep morale high. What else could you do out there apart from pray to God that you would make it back to the FOB in one piece!

As for contacting our loved ones back at home, we only got to use the phone and internet for a little while, so booking in our time slots had to be done pretty quickly, normally before going out on patrol. You never knew if you were going to make it back so every phone call was emotional to say the least.

As the days passed by the patrols kept coming; firefights were a regular occurrence and the background noise was of constant explosives (IEDs) being triggered in the distance.

This was the real deal. Just like the movies - but without all the glam.

I fucking loved it! ! !

In one firefight we were pinned down with rounds going over our heads, they literally sounded like firecrackers. My adrenaline was so high, I went to pick up my weapon by the barrel and it was red hot. I had just fired about 500 rounds through it and it was almost melting. My hand stuck to the barrel pulling the skin off. Without really thinking about it I just cracked on and laid down fire in every direction that the enemy held; firing from the hip like Rambo himself.

I thought it was as cool as fuck. My buddy was next to me doing the same, only he was armed

with a gimpy (General Purpose Machine gun) - the weapon of choice - if you want everything in its range slaughtered. A fantastic bit of kit!

I was so high. I didn't feel any pain from the burn until we got back to camp some 5 hours later.

Then it was the same detail; unload weapons, debrief and scoff; time to relax, lather myself in oil, and top up the tan.

That is "try to relax" in inverted commas, as it was difficult to totally switch off with mortar and RPGs going off all around the base. But, never a quitter, I forced myself to endure it!

I was exhausted from the firefight earlier and the patrols were really catching up on me. I was starting to miss home, my family, my son Jake (who was only 5) and my girlfriend Naiomi, BUT - as the saying goes - the show must go on - lose concentration for a second out here and things turn really ugly. We were kept on our toes by the daily reports of British casualties - many that were colleagues and friends losing limbs or even paying the ultimate sacrifice.

Worryingly, I was also losing weight on a daily basis through all the yomping and lack of calories. I think my pack now weighed more than twice my weight!

Four weeks had now passed and we had been patrolling every day; sometimes for as long as twelve hours. We had also been on guard in the towers, just to keep tabs on the base.

Listening in to the radio, hearing snipers confirm their kills was pretty fucking awesome. Often messages also told of Taliban activity. The sniper would say he had eyes on a Tal planting an

IED but, before he had time to bury it, the sniper slotted one in his head. The radio crackled "one more confirmed" and I felt as pleased as punch. At that moment in time, I felt like we were winning the war - but we weren't, the daily broadcasts told us otherwise!

The ANA (Afghan National Army) would be in the sangers with us, helping to keep an eye out. I used to look forward to working with them, mainly because they regularly brought in fresh bread, which they would share with their British friends . . . Pretty cool! However, that probably also explains the frequent trips to the toilet that all of us took the following day.

There was a time up in the sanger one evening when I got the galloping trots - I had a sudden urge to take a shit; but before I left the sanger I had just enough time to brief the ANA.

I explained, as best I could, that if I didn't go to the toilet straight away that I would crap in my pants. Then I left as fast as my legs would take me. The loo was a good 5 minutes away, even more in the pitch darkness of this blackout night, I arrived at the thunder box and placed the poo bag, that we had been supplied with, over the hole. As I sat down in great relief, I realised I was not alone . . . a huge camel spider was staring at me, LITERALLY in my face! If I hadn't already been shitting myself, I would have shat myself again!!!

In the dinge, I could hear movement, I scanned the area as best I could, there were lizards all over the floor AND even more spiders These toilets were like a bush tucker trial from "I'm a Celebrity" (no joke) . . . Get me out of here !!! I ran back to the guard tower as fast as I could! To my relief the ANA was still there and awake (not asleep as usual!)

At 0300hrs my stag was over, so I took a brisk walk back to my bed. I was really ready for this. In the gloom I could just make out the outline of my bed. I dropped my kit on it and climbed in.

A deep slumber was just about to take me under when, for the second time that night, I heard something running around. . .I strained to see in the dark what it was, when I heard it squeak! A RAT! There was a rat in my tent! I shit myself AGAIN and jumped out of my sleeping bag, nearly waking up the rest of the team. The rat vanished into the shadows, so I checked the bed over in case he had any friends that wanted to join me! Once I was certain that I didn't have their company, I got back into bed and was asleep in less than 2 minutes

This place was hell on earth; SO-O-O comforting to have 5-star accommodation.

CHAPTER THREE

BIG MISTAKE

Day 32 in the Green Zone, the heat was killing me, the dust was pissing me off AND I was absolutely exhausted from the patrolling, the firefights, and the stagging every night, BUT, as always, we were there to do a job; to get the hearts and minds of the locals. What did they want us to do? Sometimes they would talk to us, but mainly they wouldn't. That was fine as it meant that we weren't sitting ducks in the crosshairs and reach of the Taliban.

The day dragged on - we must have been out about 5 hours. We'd had the occasional gun fired at us, plus the eerie sound of bombs being dismantled by the EOD (explosive ordinates disposal) constantly in our ears! We hoped that this was by controlled detonation; not by local forces triggering one with their feet; cos that meant only one outcome!!!

As we made our way through the war-ravaged valleys of Afghanistan, we came to an abrupt stop, we heard the Taliban over the radio saying that they had eyes on our patrol! This sharpened our concentration!!!

Normally this would result in a firefight, but the Taliban were generally useless in these; being the Taliban they would fire a few pot shots off and just hope for the best. Their other tactic, and the only way they could ever get the upper hand was with their IEDs, specifically planted on a path that we frequently used. That was why we constantly changed our routes and ALWAYS had a Vallon at the front of the patrol.

It must have been around 1900hrs when we headed back to camp. I thought to myself that I couldn't wait to get this heavy ass kit off my back and relax back at camp. It was starting to get really dark and what had begun as a two-hour patrol has turned into an all-day shift; pretty unbearable in 50-degree heat, but made much worse when we realised that the team hadn't packed any night vision in our daypacks, meaning that we had to make it back to camp virtually blind. We carefully walked in the footsteps of the team mate in front. It was SCARY! to say the least. But we had been trained for this, we put every bit of faith in our team to get us back safely. The lads with the vallons at the front did a great job.

Finally, we got back to camp and this time it was a welcome relief to go through the same old routine of unloading weapons, a debrief, scoff and a shower.

Cleaning weapons was boring but absolutely essential out here because the ever-pervading dust can easily cause you to get a stoppage and under enemy fire, that's not good - as I came to realise fairly quickly.

November the 5th - Bonfire Night: Fireworks in Afghanistan were taken to a completely different level than back at home in Middlesbrough!

I had been sunbathing that day and doing some admin around camp; washing clothes, cleaning weapons and trying to keep morale up with the lads.

I rang my girlfriend, Naiomi, who is my wife now, and I was on the phone for quite a while. It was a really hard call. She told me how she was keeping spirits up by going out with friends for food and drinks etc. and I REALLY started to miss home!

Mortars and failed were going off a lot that night, and the area became known as the IED Belt due to the enemy activity in the area.

We were totally surrounded by IEDs for a distance of about 500 metres out.

November 8th 2009 -
Another day and another patrol in the dusty heat of Helmand.

I remember getting my hair shaved off that day so I was completely bald.

I had gone to the cookhouse, and just finished an absolutely delicious dinner of curry, sausage and chips with a superb pudding afterwards, VERY tasty - when I started chatting to a colleague who was sitting at the same table. He was from the Royal Anglian Regiment and, as our conversation progressed, he offered to cut my hair for me. I looked forward to having the cooler relief under my helmet!

After this I made my way back to the tent, I got a sudden urge to call my girlfriend. I was on the phone to her for about 2-3 hours, and the lads were looking for me, but all I wanted to do, at that moment in time, was call home.

We spoke about everything, but especially what we were planning to do on my R&R, which was only in a couple of weeks' time. I was so happy at this point I hated having to say goodbye: "Love you babe and see you soon.

I will call tomorrow if I get chance!"

Still not wanting to go back to the humdrum routine, I relieved my feelings by indulging myself and calling my mum. This, however, wasn't the light relief I was hoping for; she was upset, she broke the news to me that our loving pitbull, Kane, had passed away.

That just added to the homesickness!

I truthfully told Mum that I must go, I had to be up early to go out on the ground and play soldiers. I love you and see you soon.

November 9th 2009 - 0600: Reveille. SS&S, then breakfast and prepare to move at 0800.

At the container the ammo is sorted, our kit is sorted, we were just impatiently waiting for the call to go, but after another hour there was still no call. Our adrenaline was getting the better of us. We were all getting snappy and fidgety, just sitting there wondering what was happening.

Another hour passed, and still no call to move. The patrol route had been changed a few times and now we were just itching to go. Then it came, the green light! I lead the way with another of our guys in charge of the Vallon. Every inch of the way was carefully scanned for IEDs. We had taken the same route out of camp a hundred times since arriving there so it was pretty straight forward, but also a prime objective for the Taliban.

It seemed hotter that day and more humid than usual, I was feeling the strain. My kit was getting heavier, I must have lost a stone in weight since being here. My protective glasses were steaming up, making visibility difficult. As we came to a bun line (irrigation ditch) in one of the farmer's fields, we took cover in the ditch to assess our next move. I thought I would drop to the back of the patrol when I heard a booming voice:

"ROSEY GET TO FRONT."

Immediately an extra spurt of adrenaline kicks in and "ROGER" was my immediate reply.

I walked past the lads in the ditch and I could feel every step. I was out of breath. It was painful, but I made it to the front and was then instructed to get into the tree line which stood approximately ten metres in front. I got up from the kneeling position and began to scan the area in front with a guy behind me giving me cover. I got to the tree line and said to John, my team mate behind me,

"It's as dodgy as fuck in here". I took one more step and BOOM!!!!

In that split second I knew I had triggered a pressure plate IED. The force of this IED blew me about 5 metres, my ears were ringing, I couldn't see for the dust in my face, but when the dust had settled I went into major shock. I was screaming, "HELP! HELP! HELP!!!"

The pain was excruciating, it felt as though someone was holding a blow torch to my legs. I was in so much pain it was unreal. I glimpsed over my right shoulder, to see my platoon sergeant on one knee calling it in "MAN DOWN MAN DOWN!".

I was in and out of consciousness. My team were applying critical first aid, especially tourniquets to my legs. Little did I know how bad my injuries were, I just knew I was in a BAD way. I was shouting through the haze of it all to the lads "Have I still got my Crown Jewels?""Yes" came their unified reply as I'm trying so hard to stay awake. It was so hard 'cos they had loaded me with morphine and I was fighting to stay conscious. My body was shutting down, I just wanted to sleep!

At this point I felt so warm and comfortable it was almost like watching a movie at home on the sofa and you were struggling to keep your eyes open! After the first aid had been administered, the QRF (quick reaction force) were radioed to come
and evacuate me from the area. The lads made a makeshift stretcher to carry me, but I was more

concerned about another IED going off, taking out the rest of us out.

We found out in later reports that there had been an estimated THIRTY IEDS around where I had been injured.

The QRF arrived and I was screaming at the top of my voice. I was placed in the vehicle with a medic, who was a young lady, carrying even more kit than us. She was comforting me telling me everything will be fine. My left leg was hanging over the edge of the trailer, I was in immense pain and discomfort.

When I arrived back at camp I was driven straight to the Medical Centre.

There were about 10 boys all standing there as I was admitted. I was taken into a tiny room and immediately given Ketamine to knock me out but also to stabilise me for the journey to come.

I was then put on the chopper and flown to Camp Bastion for major trauma surgery.

CHAPTER FOUR

THE DARKEST OF DAYS

I woke up in what felt like a dream. I was in a flying hospital on my way back to Selly Oak Hospital in Birmingham.

I kept drifting in and out of consciousness every few minutes.
I was in a doped state and kept mumbling "I want to ring my mum."

As I came out of my daze for a split second, I looked to my right and saw other wounded soldiers that were being treated at the same time; I counted at least four before the drugs took hold again.

We touched down in Birmingham. The back of the plane opened and the ramp lowered. I was rushed straight into an ambulance and the police escorted us all the way to the hospital. It was freezing cold.

When I arrived at the hospital I went under again, but I could still hear the nurses' voices which were very frantic and assertive. The nurses and doctors weren't sure if I was going to make it!

Then I went deeper. This time when I woke up, I was in intensive care, I didn't know how I got there, where I was, or even the magnitude of my injuries.

I was now fully awake - well for at least 20 minutes. I sat up and felt for my legs -
NOT THERE!

I laid back down and whispered to myself "I have no legs!!!"

My family began to arrive - I just wanted to see Naiomi.

I was temporarily blind in one eye, so it was difficult.

I felt a real sense of safeness. I was home!

I wasn't in that god forsaken country any longer, I wasn't bothered about my legs being missing.

I was just happy to be home.

The nurse came around and asked if I was OK and if I wanted anything? I replied; "Yes a widescreen TV and some chocolate." I was heavily dosed up on medication at this point and I was really tripping out.

She came back with a TV and some chocolate fingers. I shouted "I don't want fingers I want my fucking legs back"

I was knocked out again.

My family were waiting as I was rushed back to surgery. They paid for the best the surgeon, but even he wasn't sure if I was going to pull through.

It was a long night for my family as they waited around in disbelief, not understanding or comprehending what had happened to me, but still just happy that I had come out alive.

I was transferred to a ward where rooms and rooms of injured soldiers were lying. I was put into Bay 6 - the most critical. I was amongst lads there with no arms, no legs, severe burns, etc. It was starting to sink in just what had happened! And how bad the war in Afghanistan was.

2009 saw the bloodiest year in the Afghan war when 457 British troops lost their lives - also that year an estimated 20-30 had been wounded EVERY SINGLE DAY!

Reality dawned; it can get quite depressing when you realise the extent of your injuries. I lay there in bed with machines beeping and ringing - I had tubes coming out of my mouth, my legs, my butt. It was brutal!

However, as I looked around, I realised there were a lot more people in a far worse position than me!

That gave me hope!

As the days passed, with my family and girlfriend constantly by my side, I started to not only come to terms, but realise how fucked up I was. What was I going to do now my life was wrecked?

I was in a mess. Useless!

All these thoughts were going through my head on a daily and hourly basis.

The welfare teams would come round and reassure all of us that everything is going to be fine.

We would get MacDonalds, Dominos, KFC, etc., brought to us every day - that was great, but we were on an emotional rollercoaster! My whole life had been turned upside down, and I was starting again from scratch! Even getting a shower or changing my colostomy bag was a major effort, I had a catheter inserted because I couldn't hold my urine in either.

I had a broken pelvis, burns on my hand, a broken tail bone, no legs below the knee. I was fucked ! ! ! I couldn't see how I could ever recover from this or what my future held.

* * * * * *

The days and weeks passed in the hospital - some days tougher than others!
I was really struggling to come to terms with my injuries.

I was pushing my girlfriend and family away from me. I just wanted to be alone, with the curtains closed!

I was eventually allowed out of the hospital for the day.

I was excited and nervous; I was facing the public for the first time!

Then the staring started!

I couldn't push my chair because I was so weak and frail. Naiomi and my Mum took me to the Bull Ring in Birmingham. I bought clothes and we had tea together - it was great! But I quickly realised that I was a spectacle. I had random people coming over asking me questions; people staring, people pointing. It was SO overwhelming, I just wanted to go back to the hospital where I felt safe and at ease.

When my girlfriend, family and other visitors left on the evening I would feel so lonely, I frequently cried myself to sleep,

I would also wake up in pools of sweat from the flashbacks.

It was now December and my time to leave the hospital was fast approaching. December 6th was my discharge date.

In the car on the way home I could be as near to normal as I could be - whatever normal was.

We arrived back in my home town of Middlesbrough and went straight into my Mum's and Stepfather's pub. I sat down and everyone in there flocked towards me. My friends were there, everyone who I would want to be there was there.

I slowly sipped on a pint of lager, but the pressure got to me, I couldn't sit there any longer. I became very nervous. A great panic came over me, I couldn't bear to be in there!

My girlfriend took me to my Mum's, where we would be living until we got our own place sorted, BUT as I enter the house, I realised my Colostomy bag had burst ! ! ! It was all over my clothes! There was poo all over!

I couldn't take any more!

I broke down - my girlfriend broke down too!

We both came to realise that this wasn't going to be an easy ride.

I became more and more frustrated with myself, as all these realities sank in. I was crying at anything, even the smallest of things, but never when in company. I didn't want anyone, especially my girlfriend, to see me. I wanted everyone to think that I was this super strong Infantry soldier! In truth, I was a broken man who has just had his legs blown off and his whole life tipped upside down.

I was still waking up sweating from the flash backs, lying screaming and crying, and shivering like a frightened dog, Man this was horrible, but I had to get through it. I had to weather the storm. It really was the only way. I was not going to give up! "I have only lost my legs" I kept telling myself!

Little did I realise that the worst was yet to come! Complications like my stupid shit bag bursting in my sleep and my piss tube getting blocked leaving me in extreme pain were just the start. My girlfriend had no option but to rush me to hospital on several occasions, to get things sorted out

My good friends would call round to my Mum's house to see how I was, but I would ask Naiomi to tell them I was asleep, even though they had already seen me through the window. I couldn't bear them to see me like this; especially my close friends.

Most days, I just sat at home trying to figure out how I was going to get my life back, but I just couldn't see it. My life has been flipped upside down. I had total contempt for the changed life that I'd been given and I couldn't see a way out. I couldn't see why I should be alive.

I had lost my legs - I had lost my life - I was a "Cripple"

CHAPTER FIVE

A LIGHT (at the end of the tunnel)

It was a grateful, fateful day when one of the most important letters in my life came through the letterbox. This one asked me to attend DMRC Hedley Court, THE rehabilitation unit for WIS personnel of the Armed Forces. It was there that I would learn to walk again! As well as get fit and receive physiotherapy, etc.,

I had been told it was just like a military environment, I felt a massive rush of happiness, things were beginning to come together.

I had a new house too. I was starting to think positively again!
January 11th 2010 I was picked up by my regiment's welfare team and we set off for the great Hedley Court.

I was very nervous, not knowing what to expect or what it was going to be like for the six weeks I was going to spend there. Five hours later we arrived.

The place just looked like a massive mansion in acres of land.
As we were escorted around to the back entrance I saw blokes cutting about in wheelchairs, who had no arms and legs. There were lads with only one leg, no legs; lads with one arm, no arms.

There were all sorts of different injuries - much worse than mine. Everyone was smiling, joking, taking the piss out of each other. It gave me a huge sense of relief - it was just like being back with the lads again!

I was taken to the ward where I was given my bed space. As I wheeled down the corridor I got a real sense of the mass of injuries and deaths that the Afghan war had inflicted on the British Forces!

Next day, at 0700hrs, it was time to get up.

The usual SS&S, (well almost all, as the bag attached to my stomach had already dealt with part of this!). Afterwards, I went straight down to breakfast and you couldn't move - it was like wheelchair junction!

I loved meeting up with all the lads, even though the most common question, asked every time, was:

"So where did you get blown up?" - always the opening gambit.

As we got to know one another, we became more comfortable and started taking the piss; just like we would in the regiment.

I'm sure that part of our therapy was to keep things as normal & comfortable for us as possible, so every morning we had to be on parade at 0800hrs in the main sports hall. The nominal role would be called out: -

"ROSE"

"Yes, here Sir", rebounded my reply.

Then the day's activities would get called out.

Every Monday there was Body Pump class - I loved this (eventually) - BUT my first class was brutal! Nine weeks earlier I had been fighting for my life and now suddenly I was thrashing myself in a body pump class.

Next on my timetable was physiotherapy. This is where I met my worst nightmare! ! I liked her really, but she was a HARD woman!

Prosthetics came up next. This was the one that got me really excited, because here they would get me to walk again!

When I entered the room I could see people walking on what can only be described as robot legs. It was great! I was really, REALLY excited, but also so high on my medication, that I shouted out loud, "I want some of them!"!

The prosthetics guy came over and introduced himself. He sat me down and began measuring me and also took some casts of my legs.

YES, YES, I was going to walk again! I was going to be the old James, I was going to play football again, and do all the things I used to do!

I had a really solid, satisfying sleep that night, I hadn't worked so hard for so long. I rolled over to turn the alarm off and WOW!!!, it hit me - I could barely move, the exercise and physio had really done their stuff. I don't think there was a joint or muscle in my body that didn't ache - but, weirdly, I felt great - I felt alive again, I could feel the positivity coursing through my body (or was that the Morphine!) Either way, I was raring to go again.

Day 2 at Hedley Court started in the usual way - 0800 the roll gets called and then the beastings started all over again.

However, now I'd been given my own personal trainer and we were working one to one.

This was great, even though I knew I was going to be hanging at the end of the session! Still, I could see that this (quite correctly I'm sure) was a good thing!

I knew Dinner Time was fast approaching 'cos I was starving. I was always a good eater, but all of this training had made me more ravenous than usual.

Everyone headed off to the scoff house. The usual lads were there, but now I don't bat an eyelid at the sights of missing limbs and the wheelchair jam.

I knew that I was moving on to a different level. I was also beginning to think a lot more about the future.

After dinner, it was time to head to Prosthetics. All very exciting 'cos I was about to see my new pins for the first time AND get to stand up in them.

I had them fitted and approached the parallel bars. It felt weird BUT I DID IT!
I was standing again!!! I tried to take a few steps which was hard! - but I managed it.

There was only one way to go now Rosie!!! After you have hit rock bottom, then the only way is up. And that's where I was heading!

As the days and months passed by, I was starting to get fitter and stronger through my rehab. I was beginning to think a little clearer, and started to think about life after the military.

My Medical Discharge date was fast approaching.

I spent 4 weeks at a time in rehab and then I would spend 4 weeks at home which I found difficult.

I had nothing to I had no outlook really on life, so I would just sit at home while the better half was at workI found myself eating a huge amount of junk but never realised this was a warning sign for my mental health.

We would go out for a meal on a Friday/Saturday evening, and I would be intoxicated before we even left the house I suppose this was to hide the fact I was suffering mentally. I never really understood the whole mental health thing back then and I thought that what I was doing to my body was just something normal for any lad my age to do.

Little did I know my wife and family I was suffering really bad I only realise when I look back at it now!1

I always say this now "notice the signs within yourself"

Any severe changes to your mood diet drinking habits could be a red flag and the longer you leave it the worse it gets and it could be a matter of life or death.

CHAPTER SIX

THE BIGGEST CHALLENGE OF MY LIFE

April 14th 2014 –That date was indelibly carved in my memory - the day I was discharged from the military!

I was going to miss Hedley Court, the place that turned my life around and gave me hope!

There were a stack of emotions going through my head: - What was I going to do? Will I fit in with civilians? How will I adapt to civilian life?

After leaving school I'd hardly been a Civvy; all I'd really known was the Army, and now, after 6 years in the military, I was officially one of them - a civilian.
At first, it felt great! I was free to do what I wanted with nobody telling me any different.

However, everything soon changed. Things started to get out of control. I was drinking most days and weekends until I couldn't even say my own name. Anger issues crept in.

My emotions yo-yoed up and down and I was rapidly going downhill.
Although I knew it was bad what I was doing with the alcohol and other stuff, to me, at the time, everything seemed normal, I wasn't doing anything wrong.

Now, as I look back, I wonder as to what the hell was I thinking. My drinking, eating and attitude were completely out of control.

Fortunately, that is all in the past, and now I only wanted to look forward - that was where I was heading.

So, approximately one year after leaving Hedley, I made a life changing (& life-saving) decision - I joined Tees Rowing Club in Stockton-on-Tees
I took to rowing like a duck to water (pun)! But in 2015 I began rowing training and just a few months later I had my first indoor rowing competition. Was I nervous (yes), excited (yes), but I started to feel that whole sense of belonging coming back to me after years of abusing my body with alcohol and a terrible diet.

I finished second in my heat, which I wasn't too upset about, especially as it was my first time, and I registered a new PB for the course. I was delighted!

Even more so when, shortly after the end of the race, I was approached by some GB para development coaches, whose job it was to identify new talent. They asked me if I would be interested in joining the GB development squad; the ultimate goal being to row for GB in the next Paralympic Games.
I went home to think this over . . . I reckon it took me all of five seconds to decide to accept their invitation!!!

Although I agreed, almost immediately, I would still spend hours thinking about it. In my head it was a no brainer as I loved rowing, but then there was still a part of me saying NO, what if . . .

I would play out scenarios in my head like I always do (fucking depression). My heart would be racing, thinking about everything that could possibly go wrong.
Naiomi, though, was my rock. She only ever encouraged me, and helped me through the dark times

I knew this was a massive opportunity that I'd been given, but would I be able to deal with it - all the stress, especially if I failed?
However, I convinced myself that I had nothing to lose - so, I signed the document and sent it back to Team GB.
I texted my rowing coach, John Winton, and told him the good news. He was extremely pleased for me and told me that he couldn't wait to get stuck into the training.

We knew that everything in training would have to be ramped up and that I would have to be totally committed.

Prior to this I was training Thursdays and Sundays on the River Tees with the Rowing Club; the occasional gym session at David Lloyd's was also thrown in. Now the training was going to be twice a day, 6 days a week - I was scared, but also excited to get stuck in. I was sent a month's training plan which included other types of training that I was not used to: sessions on a rowing machine, weights, yoga, etc. as well as rowing on the water. It was intense; proper full-on training, which, although scary at first, soon became something I loved and began to thrive on.

I was totally consumed with getting fit. I was on course to represent my country (if I could reach the required standard). I never really thought too far ahead but, ever-present, driving me on, was the thought that I soon could be rowing at the Paralympic Games for my Country! That kept me more focused than ever!

Rowing really was my life, I loved, lived and breathed it - that was until the day I capsized and nearly drowned!

It had been a normal, run of the mill, training session up to that point. I sat on the pontoon after taking my legs off waiting for my coach to bring the boat over. I remember it like yesterday.

I still feel emotional as I try to write this! The dialogue went something like this:

"James, are you ready?"

"Yes" I replied.

"OK" then he dropped the boat into the water. I was sitting on the pontoon, psyching myself up for the rigours to come. I got ready to get into the boat, so off went the straps on my legs and also my fake feet.

Then, when Coach was ready, I lowered myself into the boat.
"OK. I'm ready now"

"Great! Now in your own time, James, push off with a few gentle strokes and I'll come round with the launch (safety boat)"
I remember taking just one long stroke when I heard a loud clank. Just like Afghanistan, I instinctively knew something was wrong but still carried on regardless. A split second later (but what seemed like eternity), the boat rolled over.
I panicked!!!

It felt like I was back in Afghanistan, only this time there was nobody there to help me, I was on my own - drowning - on my own - because I couldn't get out of the straps that I was attached to!

Gasping for air, all I could see was water. Water everywhere and no way out of it.
Suddenly, my head cleared, I settled down and started to think clearly. I came to terms with the fact that I was on my own, and I needed to do something for myself.

THEN my safety training kicked in.

I sculled sideways with my arms and managed to get my head above water. I took a huge, grateful, breath of air and said to myself "Relax; take your straps off and you will be fine".

It all probably only took 10 long seconds to accomplish after that, BUT, when you are trapped under a boat and death seems imminent, everything seems to take an eternity, literally!

Once I had confirmed that I was interested in trying out for the Paralympics the intense training started. As previously mentioned, it was 6 days per week, twice a day; there was time for very little else. I would be up really early every day and would work on the rowing machine or weights, or swimming, or simply walking & stretching. Everything you could think of - I was doing it!

I used to hate Mondays because it was not just a tough training day, but also tough
psychologically too! Attaching my legs at 0500 when it was cold, wet and dark outside while everyone else was still in bed was not my idea of FUN! But weirdly, I loved it, and at the same time hated it!

The build up towards yet another hard training session had my stomach churning! I didn't look forward to 30 minutes of rowing on the ERG (at just under race pace), knowing I had to improve on my previous times, even if just by one second! The whole build-up made me nervous. I would tell myself it's only 30 minutes! But I would still be fearful in case my time didn't improve, or in case I went out too fast and couldn't hold it out.

I always felt great after a session on the ERG - Once it had been completed!!!
Then, it was time to rest and recover - ready for another heavyweight session in just a few hours' time!

It was full on to say the least; but how else were you meant to achieve greatness if your training isn't great?

Life outside of rowing was non-existent. I was too tired for anything else. My whole focus was on training and improving. I couldn't afford to go out on a beano and get legless (excuse the pun)

I couldn't even go out and get a takeaway pizza because my food had to be tracked and details of my intake sent into the coaches to be analysed! It was all very strict, but it was keeping my feet on the ground and focused. I didn't want to go back to the old me drinking and doing what the hell I wanted! I needed this! I needed the focus and purpose! I was in serious training now, and my first race proper, in Peterborough, was fast approaching. Coach John and myself were single-mindedly preparing for this; nothing else mattered. What a great coach he was! But not just a coach - a friend and mentor, he really did want the best for me!

Eventually, the day arrived to head south to "The Peterborough Regatta".
I was feeling totally pumped and up for it! I wasn't feeling anxious at this point, just raring to go, and happy that I could eventually put all this hard training to the test.

The preceding days had passed slowly, but, as the competition crept closer, the nerves started to kick in. We had only a light session on the water the day before and then it was . . . Race Day!

Everything kicked off at 1400 hrs. to be exact.

My coach gave me some choice words before he let me go to the start line, "Good luck, James

AND don't forget, RELAX. Stay calm - rowing shouldn't be rushed" he said.

THEN . . . there I was, on my own!

All of coach's good advice; all of my hard work, would come to nothing if I didn't put it into action - NOW!

Slowly, I headed towards the start line for the 2000m. Gently rowing to warm up, trying to relax; which is hard when you're about to start your first ever major race in a tiny little boat on unknown water! Fortunately, the weather was great; no wind and quite sunny.

Before I knew it, I was at the start line. Nervously, I looked to my left and then my right to check out the competition. Full of the positivity that Coach instilled in me, I was mentally telling myself that this was mine; get a good start and don't rush! You can take these.

The horn blasted and, exactly as planned, I eased into my stroke. I could see out of my peripheral vision that the others were scrambling and rushing. I could hear John's voice inside my head "Don't rush, don't rush", so I gently eased up to maximum power, 1,2,3,4,500 metres, I was picking them off one at a time. Before I knew it, I was in the lead by 20 metres. My adrenaline was going through the roof - I was in front and now I could see all of my competition behind me.

This was a great position to be in, because not only was I leading, but now I could adjust my pace according to what my opponents do. My most lasting memory of this, my first win, was of my coach running the full length of the river bank, shouting and coaching me to keep going – only 200 metres left! I was absolutely spent! I had put everything into this race; all my energy, mentally and physically - I was wrecked BUT I was leading! If I was struggling, my opponents must have been feeling ten times worse!

I had won my first race!

I felt ecstatic! I was on cloud 9! All of my training had paid off! My coach's words of wisdom had proved to be invaluable.

After this first race, at Peterborough, I was still full of adrenaline on my way home. What a great feeling! I felt unstoppable! But I knew this was just the start. Training would now take on a new focus, and would be increased in terms of quality and intensity, especially since I had another race imminently coming up - BUT this was no ordinary race -

THIS was the National Championships at Nottingham. I would be racing against the best GB rowers; the elite of the rowing world. These guys had been rowing for some time and had a lot more experience than me. To say I was nervous was an understatement. But I realised this was an important stage on
my learning curve. All these races were necessary to prepare me for the Paralympic Trials in early December.

Regardless of that, this was still going to be a massive event for me and my coach, and already I was very nervous for it!

My training was going really well up to this point, I was exceptionally focused and to be constantly hitting my targets was very rewarding. I was getting fitter by the day: I could feel it! I was also mentally strong and couldn't wait for the next part of this journey! ! Onward to the Olympics!

When we arrived at Nottingham for the British Championships there was a massive, unique buzz around the place. Everywhere you looked there were famous faces. All the big names from the Rowing world were there: Redgrave (man mountain), James Cracknell, etc, etc, etc They were all there - it felt surreal!!

My race wasn't for a few hours, so I took this time to prepare. I had to get the necessary fuel inside and make sure I was fully hydrated. If this wasn't taken care of it wouldn't matter how good my technique was, I would simply run out of energy before I reached the finish line.

Then, the most difficult task; just trying to relax and conserve energy was almost impossible.

Like most other athletes I found somewhere to lie down with my favourite calming tracks coming through my headphones – but it wasn't easy! I kept thinking about the race - nerves always got me – but nerves produce adrenaline, which, if handled in the right way, can be very beneficial.

After what seemed like days, I was eventually heading towards the start line, trying to focus on my own style and technique. I could see all of the elite rowers passing me and I couldn't help but think how good their techniques were – so smooth and elegant!

But I didn't beat myself up, I knew mine was good too, but just not as good! So, I had difficulty controlling those thoughts. I was fighting hard to concentrate on my own technique, and banish thoughts about my opponents.

Suddenly, 3 -2-1 and then the horn sounded, - instantly my nerves had disappeared!

I glided away easily; constantly telling myself to stay calm, breathe and concentrate.

This shouldn't be rushed! I remember hitting the pace I wanted and going really well.

The elite rowers passed me, but I wasn't bothered, I had my race plan and I stuck to it!

Now it was just me, my boat and the elements.

That day the weather was kind. It was a little windy, but not too much. It was slightly more difficult to control the boat but not so much, it was easily manageable!

SUDDENLY, one of the other rowers entered my lane, because someone had capsized into his lane. Unnerved, he simply cruised past me, unflustered, and everything returned to normal.

I wasn't expecting to win this race; I was there to gain experience. After 5, 6, 700 metres rowed and I was still in touch with the field, I felt really pleased with my performance. Soon there was only 300 metres left in the race. It was at this point that I would normally switch up a gear and go all out for the line.
I glanced at the spectators lining the bank, and I picked out my coach, as usual yelling:

"Go James, GO". This type of support is really encouraging and gives you an extra shot of adrenaline when you're on your last legs (again, excuse the pun).

So, I hit it!

I put all my remaining energy into the last 250 metres.

I finished bleary eyed, I had no idea where the line was until I heard the horn, but I was over the line dry. I had never felt tiredness like it, I couldn't breathe. The lactic acid was burning every single muscle in my body.

Eventually I got my breath back, it took about 5-10 minutes, at the same time my brain started to function again! Now I could worry about my finishing time/place. Whatever they were though, I knew that I couldn't have tried any harder, I had done everything that I possibly could have
done!

When I found out that I had come 3rd in my heat and that there were 4 or 5 GB elite rowers in there, I was delighted! These elite rowers had been in the sport for years longer than me.

I was VERY happy! But just as important, my coach was very happy too!
This was a win-win for us – especially as I happened to get a Personal Best too; which is always good for morale and your mental strength!

When the commentary team read our names out over the tannoy, and requested that we go to the presentation area to collect our medals, I could hardly walk – but the euphoria carried me through.

All the way home I couldn't stop smiling – I think I slept with the medal round my neck that night!

CHAPTER SEVEN

IT'S A FUNNY OL' LIFE

Thanks to Jimmy Greaves for that (loose) quote . . .
which has relevance, because . . .
after my race at the National Championships everything went pear shaped!!!
You would think that I'd be really upbeat about everything but, in reality, I started to feel

REALLY anxious about getting back on the water. After having such a great race, it should have been natural to want to get rowing again out on the water - But no! ! !
Fact is often stronger than fiction: I was scared, and a huge nightmare was only just starting !

It all began with flashbacks of being under my capsized boat, struggling to get out; not able to breathe! Eventually, it would wake me up, gasping for air. On numerous occasions I would lie awake all night, just trying to think of any, and every, excuse for not going to training.

I now know that my reaction, by hiding all this, was totally wrong - but I didn't feel I could tell anybody, so I kept this all to myself - bottled up inside - festering!

Inevitably, this all manifested in poor performances at training.

Every single day got that little bit worse and I was getting increasingly more angry - not just with myself but with everyone around me.

However, regardless of everything, I kept training. My coach knew nothing about what I was going through. He, too, was frustrated. He knew I had the potential to do well but all the overthinking and constant nightmares of being trapped under the boat became too much to handle!

I had my trials for the GB team in a couple of months' time, which also became another straw on the camel's back.

I missed a few sessions on the water by making feeble excuses, but I just couldn't handle it anymore. My mental health had taken a massive hit after capsizing and everything was getting worse. Some days were worse than others, but even on good days every stroke was bringing flashbacks. I couldn't get the thought out of my head that I could go over again but this time not get out!

On one occasion, I managed to get up early for a session. Everything was fine, and I was on my way to the rowing club, when suddenly I had a major panic attack and I had to call it off. Coach was fine about it, which made me feel a lot better, but deep inside I also felt like I had let him down badly.

I was lying to everyone by keeping my situation bottled up, Regardless, however, I
still forced myself regularly to training, totally ignoring the fact that I was shaking like a leaf every time I got in the boat.

There was only about 2 weeks to my trial in December and the fact it was winter and the weather wouldn't be great for rowing was ruining my life. I couldn't relax! I just wanted to give up and tell everyone that I wasn't rowing anymore! It was constantly on my mind. It was mental torture.

The thought of looking at a boat and water at this point was tipping me over the edge,

I had a plan in my head – I would complete the trial regardless, but unfortunately as we travelled down to Caversham for the trial, the weather got worse by the mile. This just added to my fear. I hardly spoke on the way down and, when we arrived at the boat house, the weather seemed to intensify. It was increasingly windy and raining heavily. The water was like the North Sea!

The Head coach gave all the triallist rowers a briefing - this included several guys who had already represented Team GB, as well as us the guys on the development team!
He shouted against the wind: "As you can see the weather is not the best, so I will understand if you don't want to go ahead with the trial".
He asked for a show of hands, about 5-6 people put their hands up and walked away, I was thinking this is it this is

my chance to call it a day! But unbelievably, I stayed quiet and decided to go ahead with it!

What the hell was I thinking??? I was as pale as a sheet and I was having constant panic attacks even just thinking about it!
When it was time to get on the water, we made our way to the jetty and it was blowing an absolute gale. The boat was bouncing all over the place. I kept saying to myself I'm going to capsize over and over again!
It took me about 3 mins to get to the start line and, when I got there, I was trying my hardest to keep the boat still! Without exaggerating, it was like I was being dragged all over by a cruise ship. My anxiety at this point was at its peak!
3,2,1- Go... but not the adrenaline rush as before - this time everything went into slow motion.

I was shaking scared and felt like a little school boy who just wanted to be at home. This was not where I wanted to be. As usual I talked to myself: "Stay Calm; Relax" but this time it wasn't working! Stroke after stroke I was getting no closer to the finish line. My technique was bad. I was slow and I knew it. I had only one thing in my mind and that was not to capsize!

The only way I can explain what I was going through on that day was experiencing PURE HELL!

I finished the race in about 6.5 minutes, my best time is about 4.5 minutes. It was the worse race of my life; I knew it was and I wasn't bothered at all! All I wanted to do was get out of there and scream!

Still bottling it all up we went for an after race briefing on who had been selected and who wasn't and guess what? - I wasn't.

I blamed it on the weather, not on my mental health taking a beating from my capsize.
The journey home from London to Middlesbrough was the longest of my life, but I had gotten it into my head that I was going to tell my coach everything.

After a couple of days recovering, I had another light training session with the guys from my rowing club.

It was a glorious sunny Saturday morning, perfect rowing conditions. I got into the boat and I didn't feel too bad. I was taking it easy, stroke by stroke, waiting for our coach to get in the safety boat and come meet us! There were probably four of us on the water - I remember this like it was yesterday - as I approached the first bridge on the river, I hit my blades on one of the boats next to me - that same sound as when I capsized - the clunk and the bang!

I completely lost it and went off on one!

I couldn't hold it in any longer "that is it I can't do it anymore!" I shouted as I started to row back to the pontoon. My coach asked me what was wrong when he saw me teary eyed, shaking and in a state of shock but also feeling massive relief. He asked where I was going and I just said that I couldn't do it anymore.
When I got off the water Coach came over to me and said "You're as white as a sheet, are you OK?"

I told him everything.

He was in just as much shock as me, but it felt like a massive weight had just been lifted off my shoulders.

What I learned from this was that never giving up isn't necessarily the best thing to do! Always try to overcome your fears - but always speak out about your feelings. As soon as I told people of how I was feeling I could feel myself getting back to how I once was!

I didn't have to live this lie anymore!

I always said that I would try rowing again - but only when I was ready!
I still row on my rowing machine but me and the water have parted ways. To this day even looking at water makes me feel sick!

CHAPTER EIGHT
INVICTUS BECONS

SO, that was the end of my rowing career - BUT onwards and upwards, ever the optimist, I looked for another sport that would keep me moving forward AND FOCUSSED - and chose Basketball.

It just felt right! I felt great playing it! At first, while I was learning the rules and techniques, I just mucked about with my local Wheelchair BB Club. This was great; lots of camaraderie, lots of sarcasm, AND NO PRESSURE!!!

I was able to blossom without the stress. But, as you know, I thrive on the pressure, so it wasn't long before I was seeking success - and I didn't have to wait long.
for the upcoming Invictus Games in Sydney!
Was I interested ??? !!! of course I was

The trials were still a few months away but, from that moment on, I trained really hard. I was really hopeful of being selected, however, after 3 years of rejection, I didn't build my hopes too high. I prepared myself for the bad news!

My treatment was coming to an end, I had endured about 18 months of it, and now I had been told that I was now ready to face the world!

Although mental health never leaves you, I was confident that my treatment would pay off and I could go back to normal - whatever normal was in my case! The big plus, for me, was that I now had a new focus. I put everything into fulfilling my dream of competing in Sydney, to represent my Country again, this time at the Invictus Games!

Training every day and travelling around the country to meet up with other Invictus hopefuls was part of the excitement for me - I loved it! This focus, and this training, both really helped my mental recovery! Throughout the previous 3-4 years I had been fully immersed in training and thrashing myself so I could become the best version of me. THIS was nothing new! – but it helped!

The 'Games' were in October 2018 and the day of the trials was in June. The sports I'd chosen to compete in were Wheelchair Basketball and Sitting Volleyball. I would say I was pretty good at both of them, considering I'd never even attempted them before - BUT I knew I had to improve in both sports to make their respective teams!

I gave everything I had at the trials; I knew I couldn't have done anymore! Now I just had to sit and wait! Wait for the dreaded email which, from previous experience, went something like this:

"Dear Mr Rose, thank you for your interest in the Invictus Games, but we are sorry to say you haven't been successful this time . . . !"

The anticipation was intense; I was just as nervous as I ever was in my rowing competitions; I had everything crossed! I desperately hoped that this time I would be selected for these Games.

After waiting all morning for an email, I finally heard my phone ping! I was almost too nervous to read the message from the Selection Committee – but I forced myself. This time, fortunately, it read more encouragingly, ". . . thank you for your interest in the Invictus Games and for taking part in the trials! We are pleased to tell you that you have been successful ! ! ! "

I read this email over and over again, it just didn't feel real. I was happy but not convinced! After reading it continuously, it still wouldn't sink in. It was like a dream. After all the knockbacks in the previous years I was finally selected to represent my country. I couldn't wait to tell everyone, which, of course, we couldn't do - until after it had been officially announced in London a few weeks later. So, you could imagine the suspense, it was killing me!

I was absolutely delighted, and I really couldn't wait to get stuck into the training and bonding
with my new team mates in the months ahead.

As probably expected, we all gelled straight away. Our coaches, also, were great, they had lots of experience under their belts, so listening to them, and taking their advice on board, was crucial.

Ultimately, these few months of training were all we would have together before we flew to Sydney! From the time of the invite, right up to the time we were all sat in the airport going out, everything felt surreal!

It's kind of crazy what a bit of good news can do to your morale! It's like all the bad stuff that happened to me in the past back in Afghanistan seemed to have vanished, and all the bad thoughts had vanished too! I truly believe that this was down to me having a focus; something to aim for again. After I had given up on rowing because of my capsize, I never thought I would be able to get back into that kind of mindset again. This time, however, it was different. I was even more excited; maybe because there was no way of nearly killing myself by drowning, I don't know!!!

Weirdly, I never really felt any pressure; even though I had a lot to learn. I was taking
everything one step at a time, as it came, listening intently to my coach and other team members who had been playing the sport for years.
This was an ideal situation; we had a good mixture of players of all abilities! I was once again in my element; I was loving training again ! ! !

Game day arrived and the adrenalin was flowing. We were taking on the hosts!

After winning our first game against the hosts we were on a massive high - we were now to face the Netherlands! They would certainly not be push overs as they had an Olympic medalist in their squad! He was everything you would expect an elite basketball player to be; he was quick, he could move and he could score from almost anywhere, and he made everything look so easy!

Whereas I would be playing eyeballs out at 110% effort each time trying to score, hahaha!

When the buzzer sounded, it was game on!

We took the lead and scored! It was frantic - up and down the court at 100 mph! Adrenaline going through the roof! Coach yelled at me to calm down and make certain of my passes. My job was to try and keep the big guy from receiving the ball, interceptions were vital, if he got it, it would be game over!

We were neck and neck on points when the big Dutch Olympian got it on the 3-point line; without breaking sweat he casually banged a 3 pointer in with pure ease. Then, to rub salt in, he sank another, and we were now behind! However, we were still in it - we knew we could still win!!! All we had to do was get the ball up court, make the right passes. In fact, everything we had been doing in training, every session for weeks and weeks!

Easier said than done! When there are thousands of supporters screaming and the balls coming towards you at a million miles per hour, staying calm and executing this plan takes on a different dimension. This is where experience comes in. Something I didn't have, but plenty of others in the team did, they had been playing the sport for years. I put all my trust in them and followed their lead. This was only my second competitive game of basketball - talk about being thrown in at the deep end!!! It was pretty relentless to say the least, but I was thriving on it. Nobody knew it was only my second game - and I wasn't telling. BUT they might have had a clue if my shooting was anything to go by - I think they would have guessed, hahaha!!!
We remained neck and neck throughout the game until the last few minutes, then, from out of nowhere, Big Dutch got the ball and, as casually as you like, pops in another 3 pointer!

Game over UK v NED defeat.

We shook hands - thanked the crowd for their amazing support and moved onto the next match -the mighty USA !!!

OK, that was the 'easy'ish' games out of the way: next up were the Yanks. If I remember rightly, we all knew that this was going to be the toughest one yet!

The Americans lived and breathed basketball. This was their game! Just as us Brits invented football the Yanks invented and developed the game of Basketball to a high level. They had some real quality players but I was

confident we could still be triumphant! The experience that we had in our squad (barring me, lol!) would see us through. OK, I was a beginner but I was improving rapidly!
This was the BIG one!!! The reason why we were here, to take on the best, and none were bigger than the USA.

We had a few hours training leading up to this make-or-break match and we all felt good. All of our team gelled, and were operating like a well-oiled machine. We all had a lot in common which made training a whole lot easier, with the banter and joking ever present. This meant we were all relaxed, even though this was the biggest game we had all played in. We would lose there and then if we didn't have this attitude - we wouldn't progress to the final. Everyone wanted to make the final (you'd be a liar if you said otherwise). We all wanted to win and win only! Nothing else would cut it!

The ball was in the air and Big Rich, our forward, jumped for it. The tension was immense.

They scored first, but we came straight back and matched them - it was gripping, proper end to end stuff. The crowd was right behind us and screaming. Everyone wanted the Yanks to be beaten. It made the start tense, but you tend to block all that as you concentrate on your job in hand.

After five minutes had passed the electric atmosphere was interrupted as our coach called a time out. He wanted fresh arms and heads on court and also to make a few tactical changes.

Both teams were scoring freely, but they had this big guy who was smashing 3 pointers for fun.

We couldn't get close to him! As soon as he was allowed to get in range, BANG, he sank another 3 pointer. Gradually, we started to slip behind!
We were still confident that we could turn this one around; we just had to get the ball to our big forwards who would finish it. However, this was easier said than done, the Yanks were all over us, like tramps on chips. It was hard and they knew they had the upper hand.

They were relentless, we were slowly slipping away, totally at the mercy of the USA. We scored a few more and appeared to be bringing the game back, but they just ground on! They were

clinical. Every time we scored they merely stepped up a gear to pull one back! The final score was something like 52-40 to the USA.

It was a great game, and we knew we had played a great team. We couldn't dispute that the better team won on the day. We shook hands and once again thanked the supporters, and then headed back to the dressing room for our usual team talk. We were all a bit deflated. If we had won this match we would have been guaranteed a silver or gold medal in the final - but now we had to beat New Zealand in the third-place final, to take a medal home!

We knew what was at stake, lose and we'd go home with no medal. Losing was not an option!

Team spirits were high, we were determined and nervous, but this only added to the adrenalin as we took to the court.

The whistle went, this was it! Physically and mentally challenging, the play flowed back and forth, as both sides scored. The crowd was incredible, we could hear the cheers and screams and this drove us on. Minutes to go and we were in the lead, could we hold onto it?

YES! YES! YES! The whistle went! We'd done it! We'd overcome all the adversity, we'd achieved bronze medal! My heart was racing, the euphoria I felt was visible for all to see. I had achieved something amazing, I had been part of a team again, a team of people who, like me, had faced all the challenges put in front of them and had come out the other side as winners. There is no feeling on earth to describe how incredibly proud I felt.

CHAPTER NINE

CLIMB EVERY MOUNTAIN

The Invictus Games were now nearing their end, and I was exhausted!!! - but still on a massive high!

It was quite a surreal experience, representing your country at such a massive event, but at the same time competing in something you love.

I was already thinking about what I was going to do with myself next, because although these

Games were almost over and done, within just a couple of weeks they had totally consumed me, and for the best part of a year had been my whole life, through training camps and arduous training off my own back.

I was scared! Scared that I would lose myself again as a result of not having that purpose or goal any more. Deep down, however, I knew that I would find something else to focus on. For me, having that purpose and goal to work towards really helped with my mental health – it kept me on the right track.
So, whilst spending nearly a full day travelling home from Sydney, I had time to think!

What do I do next?

Still on a high when I got home, I switched on the TV and almost the first thing that I saw was a documentary about Mount Everest.

That was it ! ! ! I was going to climb Everest!

I had always been pretty obsessed with Everest anyway, (or climbing any other mountain for that matter), but Everest was the ultimate badass mountain! I could look at it all day and not get bored. I have watched just about everything out there about this magnificent mountain, so when I saw the show on TV called "Extreme Everest with Ant Middleton" I was once again hooked - I had to watch it. The sheer beauty of the mountain and the respect it demands to climb it is breathtaking. I had gained so much confidence back in my life after competing in the Invictus Games, that I literally thought I could take on the world and anything that was thrown at me.

After the show had finished, I immediately upgraded my Facebook status to state that "I would love to climb Mt Everest" - One day hey!!!???

Within about 30 minutes of the post going out, one of my friends from the Games, Darren, got in touch and said to me, "Why don't we climb Kilimanjaro instead?"

I agreed straight away, and we left it like that.

I never really thought much of it to be honest. I told my wife what my plans were and a few other family members. They were all very sceptical, and thought I'd finally lost it! They didn't believe that, in my mind, because I had agreed to it, I was going to do it!

Secretly, I thought I might be going crazy too! I told myself that it would never happen but it's good to dream. I needed that focus back in my life and to set a challenge up for myself to keep me on the right tracks. This was certainly going to do that!

The projected date we set was sometime in 2019 - the back end more than likely - to give us time to train. This had only been our initial conversation - when nothing else transpired, I just forgot about it.
After a few weeks had passed, all thought of climbing Kilimanjaro had gone, when, out of the blue, I got another call from Darren - the first time since our conversation 3 weeks earlier - and everything stepped up a gear again!
"James," he said, "I have been doing a few things to prepare us for the trek up Kilimanjaro."

I was like . . . eh!

My heart started pounding out of control!!!

Really, I had begun to think that this was just a pipe dream and nothing else. But, unknown to me, Darren had already been planning this trip for more than a year, BUT as it failed to take off -due to unforeseen circumstances, he shelved it! So, he already had a few contacts in place when he asked me again "SO - are we doing this then or what?"

I thought about it for a millisecond, and said "Yes, sod it! Why not? Let's go for it!"

Now that I was definitely in, I completely winged it to the max! I began training and telling the world what I was doing. There were exciting times ahead . . . but I was also shitting myself!

I was about to attempt to climb the highest free-standing mountain in the world – unaided –

AND I had no legs ! ! !

As the cogs of motion started to whir, my brain kicked into gear!

First of all, I had to get some new legs capable of completing this trek. So, I booked a trip to the prosthetics department to get some made to measure, then I could, and did, begin training,

My training consisted of weights, cardio, AND getting out onto the hills of the beautiful North Yorkshire Moors, which were just on my doorstep. When I needed something a bit more demanding and higher, I could drive over to the Lake District in about an hour!

The Lake District!!!

I was absolutely 100% into this now!

I WAS BUZZING!

I had one year to train for it.

Everything started off slowly to begin with – but it was all useful. I was getting out on local walks, mainly on the Moors, where I could try out all sorts of different walking aids. I went up and down hills, trying to work out what was the best equipment, and also what was the best way of using it.

I was literally, at times, crawling on all fours, when I suddenly realised that THIS technique was in reality the best one to use. It was exceptionally good when it came to the boulders. I could just crawl over them like a monkey!
It took me 3-4 hours the first time I went up to Captain Cook's monument on the Cleveland Hills, which is only 2km in total, up and down - nothing really - but I was on such a high after completing it, especially after being out in the fresh air for so long with the magnificent views over this countryside! It was exhilarating!!! In my opinion, you just couldn't beat it being out in the wilds of North Yorkshire – even when I was piss wet through - tired and sore - I just loved it!

I just couldn't wait for my next outing!!!

After climbing up to the 'monument' - which I hadn't done since I was a kid when we used to camp up there and get into mischief - I was now aching from head to stump!

Incredibly, it wasn't much more than just a little walk in comparison with what was to come, so I knew I had to up my game and aim to get out at least twice per week!
I started getting up early, 0500 sometimes, and got out on the North Yorkshire moors to train, but I knew in the back of my mind it wasn't enough! Yes, this hill training was a good start, BUT I needed mountains!

I knew where I needed to be, and that was the Lake District, where there are some of the biggest mountains in England, but my first step towards the mighty Lake District and beyond was going to be Roseberry Topping! If you're from the North East you will probably have seen it many times, it stands out a mile and is a beautiful looking thing. I couldn't wait to get involved with it and climb up it again.
I had found a few training partners at this point; all veterans and all part of the same regiment! John Gilpin, Ray Priest and the man mountain Gerry Garvey - you know you're in safe hands when Gerry's around! Likewise, John Gilpin, who was my welfare officer when I got injured. He was the one who informed my mother and family what had happened and ever since that day we have remained great friends. As for Ray (Oz), I met him through John. He was suffering with his mental health and we agreed that getting out walking together would benefit everyone but especially support me and get me up these bloody mountains!

It was a cold, wet, miserable northern morning, much too early at 0800am, when John, Oz and myself met up at the

bottom car park near Roseberry Topping. We began the hike up. It took me about an hour to get warmed up before I could stop moaning and bitching to myself, and start to enjoy the climb. I slipped all over the place, crawled up the hill and blew out my ass. I knew this had to be done; I couldn't do anything about it, I had agreed to it, so I wasn't going to let anyone down - especially me! I could see the top, it was so close, yet still so far away. I was overflowing with adrenaline, because I knew I was going to summit Roseberry Topping – this was a HUGE
achievement for me!

We'd made it to the top! We stood there taking it all in! It was pissing down but I still had a massive buzz on!

After I'd got some food and some warm coffee down me, I started the descent, back to the car.

I couldn't stop smiling as I thought about what I had just accomplished! But still I knew I had to improve on the 3 hours I had just taken to get up this moderate hill! Everyday hiking in Kilimanjaro would be 10-15 hours so I had to massively up my game.

I went out the following week and smashed it! Just under an hour !!!

I was gaining confidence fast and felt great! The guys were now talking about the Lake District (Helvellyn) which is no joke! At this point I was just agreeing knowing I had to do it. I had to test myself on something really big, and Helvellyn was going to be the ultimate test.

I was really confident but shitting myself at the same time.

The mountains needed to be respected, especially for someone like me who felt completely out of my depth and vulnerable to the elements - but that's what excited me. I loved the outdoors, being wet and muddy, scared and pumped!

Helvellyn stands at 950m tall - it's a monster by British standards, but Kilimanjaro is more than 5 times higher at 5885m. However, the weather on Helvellyn can still change in an instant and mild conditions can suddenly become dangerous.
We set off from the camp site and immediately it was full on. We were straight into it. As I said before, it takes me 1-2 hours to really hit my stride and forget about the pain I had from blisters and moaning. I hate talking to anyone during this time because I feel pissed off with myself.

Doubting myself and always contemplating giving in straight away. However, I knew my body and I knew that this rough patch would pass, I just needed to dig deep!

We'd been going 3-4 hours; I could just about see the summit through the mist when the weather turned. Wind and rain shrouded the top. It was bad! We heard that an oldish man had been blown off Striding Edge, which was pretty brutal to say the least.

I felt vulnerable and out of my depth.

The team made a command decision to turn back due to the time of day. It would have been pitch black on the way down and that would have been too dangerous, especially for first timers like me.

I felt like a failure, I felt shit! I really started to doubt myself all the way back to the car. We all discussed attempting it again in better weather and I agreed straight away.

Yes, yes, but when!!

A few weeks passed and we were there again! We stayed at a hostel this time, which also had the advantage of being 500m closer than the camp site. This give us a little extra time to reach the summit - but the weather again was fucking brutal! Rain and wind all the way up!

It took about 4.5 hours to reach the summit and all I wanted to do was scream, curl up into a ball and sleep. I had no other choice but to keep going. There was only another 500m to go (all up hill on slippy rocks and gravel) but I was tired, wet and cold and completely pissed off! I kept telling myself 'Nobody is carrying you, nobody is coming for you, it's all you!'

Finally, I reached the flat at the top of Helvellyn! The wind was so strong that I was getting blown off my feet! Horizontal wind and rain battered the trig point so I got into a sheltered position as fast as I could. After sitting down I knew I had it all to do again and that was the most

demotivating thought process I could think of. I was absolutely spent! Tired, aching, sore; the only way I was going to get down was by moving forward very slowly, one step at a time. I told myself just to 'keep moving, keep going, almost there James, think of the feeling at the bottom of
the mountain!' That was my mantra, the driving mechanism that was my focus. After nine and a half hours of long, emotional, draining, aching, wet and physically demanding effort, I could see the white bonnet of my car in the car park. That was one of the best feelings I have ever felt in my life!

I did it! I had climbed HELVELLYN (at the second time of asking!)

Motto: - NEVER GIVE IN!!!!

After climbing Helvellyn I was again on a massive high for days! The feeling was of huge accomplishment. I was buzzing!

We were nearing H hour - exactly 2 months before we climb the mighty Kilimanjaro.
Daz was the main man behind everything, he had been working hard to get all the final things in place, when I got a phone call from him:"Right, that's it, no turning back now!

The flights are booked and we leave in mid-September !"

My heart sank for a few moments and I began to panic!!! But then I regained control. I took a few deep breaths, gathered my thoughts and instead of thinking of all the things that could go wrong, I thought of the great adventure I was about to commence –

AND ALL THE THINGS THAT COULD GO RIGHT!

Up to that point I had only met one of the guys who was climbing with me, and that was Daz, the guy who put the whole thing together. He lived in Kent, like the rest of the team, and I hadn't done a single training session with any of them. This was a slight concern to me because when I was out hiking I always needed some sort of support. Would this team be able to adapt to this?

When the full team eventually got together my worries were quickly eased, two of the team were ex forces, so improvisation and adaptation came naturally to them, due to their military background. We were all Brothers in Arms and lived by the same motto "Improvise, Adapt and Overcome."

Although we hadn't met each other in person, up to now, we had always been just a phone call away, and we had all spent the previous months doing our bit to help. That could have been just sending emails, getting sponsors for our chosen charity, organising stuff, or simply training but it all added up to a massive commitment!

We had been getting a lot of publicity up to flying out: Sky News, Good Morning Britain, This Morning, 5 News, BBC News, ITV News and all the major newspapers!

We never thought it would gain so much attention - but it did! Simply by being invited to attend all of these meant that we were doing something of national interest. Also, we achieved our main aim and started to get more donations towards our cause and ultimately raise awareness of mental health!

Often, after a full day of live interviews, I was pretty exhausted, so when I began my long journey back to Middlesbrough it was inspiring that, when I was waiting at Kings Cross station, a complete stranger approached me and pushed £20 into my hand, saying, "I have just seen you on TV, Good Luck! - I felt great and loved - the whole country knew about our monster challenge!

I had a few more training sessions to get in before I once again returned to London the following month. I had to keep myself ticking over, even though I knew I had done everything I could -

Maybe I could have climbed a few more mountains - but I knew I was ready!

Throughout my life I'd always winged my way, just like most other people, and that's exactly what I felt I was doing here; winging it to the top of highest free-standing mountain in the world! ! !

I said my goodbyes to my family and friends and I set off for London- I spent my last weekend there with Naiomi. It brought back a lot of emotions, like when I was in the military and felt that shot feeling in the stomach when you have to go somewhere that you really don't want to!

I knew I had to do it. I wanted to do it, and, although I was shitting myself, I was super excited at the same time!

'If I can do Helvellyn then I can manage Kilimanjaro, right?'

Nothing was going to stop me now!

I turned up at Gatwick airport with all my mountaineering kit, PLUS a massive bag of spare legs!

I felt massively out of my depth. That feeling melted away though when the team arrived - the first time we had met in months. For some of us it was the first time ever!

We all clicked straight away, which was what I had been worried about. Marco, Daz's best mate, was an instant morale booster with his jokes and humour, which I knew we would need when the shit hit the fan. He was ex RAF, like Daz, so there was always a bit of banter going with us, as there always is between the Army and the Brylcreem Boys; but it was all harmless and good character building - I'm sure!?!

Our camera guy, Louis, was great! Laid back and very handy with his camera, capturing a lot of memories.

Mel, Daz's wife, was the motivator in the group. A great help to me! Always on hand when you needed her!

Our team was a great mixture of personalities, which all seemed to come together nicely!

Everything was so relaxed, and everyone was happy and excited. We had a quick bite to eat and then distributed all the kit which North Face had provided as part of our sponsorship deal with them. Then – the real buzz started as we made our way to Departures.

Lift off to Tanzania 1400, ETA 2345 (nearly a 12-hour flight)!

CHAPTER TEN

NO TURNING BACK

OK – This was serious now - **Absolutely NO TURNING BACK.**

The flight was 30,000 feet in the air when I went through the whole gamut of emotions – excited, dry mouth, sweaty palms, shitting myself!

What if I fail - what if I can't do it - what if I'm too unfit – Will I be able to follow this mammoth challenge through to the end?

If I failed, I would be letting everyone down . . . AND I didn't want to end up in that big black hole again!

All of these thoughts, and more, were rushing through my head at a million miles an hour. It was unbearable to say the least, so much so that it knocked me out, and when I woke up we were on our descent to a landing strip in Tanzania.

On leaving the airport, what struck me first was the sheer poverty that the locals were living in -but the smiles on everyone's faces were absolutely amazing!

It was about one and a half hours commute to our hotel, where we'd arranged to meet our guides for the duration of the stay. We also needed to check that ALL of our kit had arrived and as for myself, check that my legs weren't going to malfunction – 'cos to fail half way up a mountain would be my worst nightmare!

I made sure I had everything I needed (probably had too much) but, as I hadn't done anything like this before – better to have too much than too little!!!
It was like being back in the Army in training; day one week one - Shit loads of kit and not knowing what to do with it!

It took me a few hours, but finally I reckoned I had everything that I needed; spare legs, spare feet, warm clothing, waterproof clothing, spare gloves, spare parts for my legs, everything! I was all packed and ready to go! AND we still had a couple more days before we set off!

I was pretty quiet before leaving! No matter how hard I tried, all I could think were bad thoughts
– all the what ifs… But, I reckoned, that this was all part of the journey, so I just sat quietly, and contemplated, miserably!

My adrenaline was going crazy! I just wanted to get cracking and begin the five-day trek! I knew that once I got started my game face would be on, and then there would be no stopping me!

My adrenaline was going crazy! I just wanted to get cracking and begin the five-day trek! I knew that once I got started my game face would be on, and then there would be no stopping me!

It took nearly two hours to reach the starting point of our trek, and it was the longest two hours of my life. When we arrived, the locals unashamedly stared at me. I could read their minds, they were thinking 'what the hell is he doing - is he crazy?' Maybe I was - but I wasn't here for them,

I was here to do one job and that was to climb their mountain, and I was determined that I wasn't going to waste this trip by failing! ! !

The first part of the trek was through jungle and, since I was not a big fan of creepy creatures, spiders and all that type of stuff, I really wasn't looking forward to the next few days!

A quick brief with the full team, and we were off!

Just like Helvellyn a few weeks ago - BUT this time for 5 days!

Day One
We set off on our gruelling challenge (for me anyway) when it suddenly sank in - this was going to HURT.

We were already at quite a high altitude, and I could feel my breathing wasn't quite right - but I cracked on anyway and, after 1-2 hours, when I was fully warmed up, as I acclimatised to the conditions, it became much better.

As we trekked through the jungle, monkeys were swinging from tree to tree and spiders the size of my head crawled past my face.

Now, I'm an absolute fairy when it comes to spiders or anything like that, (anyone who knows me would verify that) - but for some reason this time they weren't bothering me! I think this was because my Army training had kicked in – I was in combat mode, and I was giving my total concentration to the task in hand.
I walked 'normally' for much of the time but occasionally had to monkey crawl as I adapted to the steep terrain!

As the day went on it got darker and colder really quickly. After 5 hours of hiking through the jungle we were completely submerged in darkness and the jungle came to life. At this point I was getting really tired, which I knew was going to happen, but all I wanted to do was reach the first checkpoint.

It was a steady incline up to the first hut on the Marangu route, but as 6-7-8 hours flew by, there was still no sign of our first stop! All I could hear was '500m and we are there - 30 minutes and we are there – etc,' I just kept crawling along, muttering to myself and getting really pissed off. I was tired, wet and hungry, but kept going by telling myself 'keep going, keep going, keep going -one step at a time, keep going'.
Then I saw it; a faint light in the distance which I knew was the first stop. nine and a half hours of jungle creatures, mud, sweat and the occasional close encounter

with HUGE spiders - but we made it! The jungle was behind us now, but it's not all over, our journey had just begun.

As I sat there eating dinner, adrenaline was coursing through my body! However, I knew I couldn't get carried away - that was only day one! There were still 5 days to go to reach the summit and I was desperate for a sleep.

At this point my legs were fine, I hadn't got any blisters and I was in good nick. My body was tired, but my mind was strong - which was, ultimately, what would get me through this challenge more than anything! I had a quick check of my kit and tried to get some sleep as we were up in just five hours for round 2.

After 9 hours of slogging it out on the first day, each day after was going to get tougher with blisters, altitude, fatigue and just the general negative thought of giving up. This was where I needed to dig into my mental reserves - resilience and power would get me through this energy sapping grind!

We all have this capability; it's just learning how and when to use it!
It's a challenge for a reason - a challenge which was not meant for amputees like me, but I was going to succeed and overcome every obstacle! The ground was shit, it was steep, it was horrible but I was doing it!

Day Two
I woke up feeling good and ready to go, however, first, I had my own personal mountain to climb – the toilet !!!

We were carrying a portable toilet with a little tent over it for privacy. It was very basic, but it was either use that or squat and crap in a hole in the ground – now for obvious reasons I can't squat (hahaha) - so the portable loo it was then!

That, however, was a challenge in itself!

I only had my little stubby legs with me, but I needed to completely remove them and then almost do a Fosbury Flop High Jump to get on top. Accomplishing all of this without tipping the toilet over was another obstacle! One which would have disastrous, smelly results if I failed!

The toilet would also have been quite full at this time of the morning, so failure was not an option.

HUGE credit to the porters, who would clean and empty it every morning and every night, without grumbling – (rather them than me!)

After breakfast, we set off.

"Here we go" I mumbled to myself, "Let's do this."

I just wanted to see the mountain in all its glory, but I wasn't able to, just yet, as we still had a bit more jungle to work through, AND it was getting hotter!
Even through the dense forest you could feel the sun burning, but soon we'd be out of it, and then what?

When, we emerged, the sun REALLY hit us! ! ! But that faded into insignificance as we got our first glimpse of this amazing mountain that we were going to climb. Pictures of it on the internet had been amazing, but to see it in real life was, in the true sense of the word, AWESOME.

NOW it REALLY sunk in that this was going to be a mammoth challenge; MORE mammoth than I had initially realised!

As the crow flies, Kilimanjaro was about 2-3 hours away, but the dead ground which we needed to cover would make that at least 2-5 days! I took every metre of it in my stride, trying to find some sort of rhythm which I could stick to and gain some ground - but it was tiring - not just because of the heat, but also because of the amount of water breaks we were taking. However, I knew these were vital if we were to stay hydrated – an absolute must even on smaller mountains than this!

"Pole Pole" the guides kept telling us (which means slowly, slowly). They were obviously concerned that the group was attacking this first part too aggressively, and would run out of energy before reaching the summit. Now that just suited me, going slowly would help me when we got higher up because it would give me more time to acclimatise.

We reached a checkpoint after about 8-9 hours and I desperately needed to re-fuel and evaluate my blisters (which at this point were getting really big and sore due to the heat and sweat in my sockets. My stumps had been moving around too freely up to now, and this caused friction! The pain of the blisters actually took the tiredness away as I never thought of it!

After a quick stop for food we set off again, the temperature had dropped suddenly and dramatically. I didn't really feel the cold because my heart rate never dropped below 120bpm,

but I could tell it was biting because of the reaction of the others in the group. I felt bad, seeing this, as I was basically the pacesetter. They couldn't go any faster than I was able to. This began to play on my mind so I tried to speed up so that we could reach camp faster, but all that was doing was tiring me out quicker and making me depressed about the situation!

The more I thought about the others the more angry I got, as I knew they could all go faster and be warmer, but it was me who was causing the group to go slow!

I would regularly tell them to walk on and leave me and I would see them at camp! But there was no way they would allow that to happen! We set out as a team and we would complete each day as a team! So as a team, we struggled on!

It became pitch black again very quickly and I'm sure that some of the guys were getting really pissed off with me asking, every 100-200 metres or so, "How far is it now, how far?"

After 12-13 hours of trekking through blistering heat, then going into dark freezing cold, we were ALL pissed off!

We were each going through several litres of water, so much so that one of the guides ran on ahead to re-fill our water supplies; then he'd run back with it for us! What a guy - these guides were phenomenal, REALLY made of strong stuff!

After 14 hours I could once again see lights in the distance. - This was Camp number 2!

I tried to go quicker but I was absolutely done in. My legs were bleeding and my hands were swollen due to all the crawling I had been doing - my body was running on empty.

I will never forget this stage, because as we came into camp there was a cabin right at the edge -but the kitchens and our hut were about another 500m away. I told the team to leave me there; I would sleep at this point as I couldn't walk another 500m! When they refused I took a massive strop - I was completely spent and angry, BUT they insisted that I had to go on.

They were right!!! Deep down I knew I HAD to make it to the kitchens and re-fuel. There were no two ways about it; there were no wheelchairs here, and nobody to carry me - it was all down to me . . . and all I wanted was my bed!

At dinner we had a discussion about the next day; which would, fortunately, be an
'acclimatisation day'. This meant the team would walk1000-2000m and then back to camp again - I instantly said I was not doing it - I would be fine without it.

I was in more need of rest. My legs and my blisters were excruciating and sore. The team agreed and only a few went further up to get the much-needed acclimatisation.

Day Three
I spent the whole day in the hut, resting and refuelling, and gathering my thoughts. After a good day's rest I knew I would be ready for the penultimate day before we reached base camp!

I couldn't really feel any adverse effects of altitude at this point. My breathing was, considering the conditions, quite good, but what I did notice was it felt like I had a fridge on my back. I was completely weighed down by my pack! It made everything feel like hard work, my legs turned to jelly.

I knew that the next couple of days were going to be an absolute nightmare but I had nothing else in my sights – I had to reach that summit!

Day Four
I remember setting off for base camp, which was just a measly 9-10 hours of hiking, over shit terrain for an amputee! Surprisingly, for some bizarre reason, I felt absolutely great - not physically but mentally – which

meant that I could just push on without any shit thoughts running through my head!!! That little guy wasn't tapping on my shoulder telling me to stop! I felt as though I could just keep going.

'What's going on?' I mumbled to myself, feeling quite chuffed.

I wasn't moving quickly, but the key here was that I wasn't stopping as much as previously -which gave me the encouragement to keep pushing on. One foot in front of the other, I was gradually chipping away at this monstrous task.

I don't think I spoke to anyone the whole way to base camp, I was completely in the zone! I was purely focussed on slogging it out - I was getting sore but I had the mental strength, this time, to just brush it off.

I think this had always been part of my make up, but now I had taken it to another level, and I had honed it more precisely over the last few days.

We crossed open ground which was like a desert and Mars all rolled into one! The wind was strong and coming in sideways, I began to feel completely out of my depth, but I wasn't stopping - the only thing that would stop me now was if my legs fell off (pun intended!)

Six to seven hours had passed and it was time to sit down for some dinner – which, amazingly, we were supplied with each day by our incredible guides and porters. It was nothing fancy, just a scabby bit of chicken, a boiled egg, some juice and a bar of some sort. However, being the fussy bastard I am, I left it; and tucked in to my Kendal Mint Cake energy bars - plus the very essential water, of course!

I really wanted, this time, to reach base camp in daylight. As you know, all previous days we had arrived at camp in pure darkness.

This time, as we approached the camp, we began to see other climbers being carried down the mountain due to severe altitude sickness!!! This was worrying, but somehow it made me even more determined to complete this challenge. I was devoted to the task BUT, at this moment in time, all I could think about was getting into my bed!
I had been getting extremely tired and pissed off. I was sore and the blisters were getting worse I just wanted to curl up in a ball and sleep!!!

As we gradually got closer to camp, we became completely immersed in the magnitude of the whole environment - this mountain was huge! AND steep!!! When you see pictures of Kilimanjaro, you think 'WOW, that looks great!'- but when you are literally stood at the bottom of it, looking up, it is mind blowing! Completely different - steep and never ending!!! I had butterflies.
We arrived at base camp around 20:00hrs, after 9-10 hours, the hut we were in was like Piccadilly Circus! It was so busy with other people preparing to reach the summit that we had no room to sleep. It took a lot of persuasion to finally get what we wanted but, eventually, we had our own room, with just our team sleeping in it,

and not a load of other people from every corner of the world!

The guides from each team were going round everyone in their group with a little machine to check on oxygen levels. If it registered below a certain number then they wouldn't let that person continue, for their own safety.

My heart sank! I really thought that this was where my adventure ended. I felt tired; I had a pounding headache; I was sore and pissed off. I could have murdered someone at this point –BUT imagine my elation when I passed the test!!!

But now, I REALLY, REALLY needed sleep - we were due to attempt to reach the summit in less than three hours! I desperately needed rest, WE ALL NEEDED REST!

The excitement had got my adrenaline pumping, sleep wasn't going to come easy, so, I calmed myself down by ripping old blister tape off and applying new. I had to be prepared as best as I could 'cos this was going to be a big fucking task!

I'd made it this far by sheer determination, NOW I just needed to keep moving forward, one step at a time, and concentrate on the end goal - that's all - nothing else in the whole world mattered now!

I got into my doss bag and, amazingly, very quickly drifted off into a deep sleep!

SUDDENLY; BANG, BANG, BANG!!! The light was blinding! "LET'S GET READY!!!

Thirty minutes and we are off!!!"

Day Five

It was freezing!!! I just wanted to stay in my sleeping bag - but, yet again, training kicked in - 3-2-1 - I jumped out of my doss bag and was quickly dressed and ready to go.

I remember putting my legs on and they were absolutely FREEZING cold! It was excruciating when my inner liners touched my blisters! I just knew it was going to be one of those days, so I put my legs on as quickly as possible and began walking around the hut to warm them up!

I also needed some hot food and drink before we went out. I expected the guides, with their usual clock-work efficiency, to bring some through the door!!! BUT NO! - they brought tea and coffee BUT no food!

We needed fuel!!!

THEN they came in with popcorn! I started laughing to myself but took a handful anyway! I stuffed some in my pack, stuffed some in my face, then drank some very welcome, warming
coffee . . . Then it was time!

I made my way outside. It was pitch black. The only lights to be seen were the head torches of other nutcases, climbing up and down the mountain.

I looked at my 4-foot-tall frame, then I looked at the silhouette of this absolutely huge mountain, and I gulped. It took my breath away.

It was 0100 hrs and I was seriously questioning life!?!? What was I doing !!!!!!!!!!!

As I stood there questioning my life, all I wanted to do was get to the top of this monster. It is very rare that this happens, but sometimes it's at times like this that I wish I had legs, so I could just run up this bastard thing. Then I took a hold and told myself: 'You haven't! and you can do fuck all about it; so suck it up buttercup and get cracking, you set yourself this challenge, now bloody well finish it!'

Climbers continued to be dragged past me due to their severe altitude sickness. They literally couldn't stand up and were throwing up as they were being dragged down by the guides. Head torches could be seen in the distance moving slowly.

It was just before dawn, and you could only just make out the imposing outline of this
magnificent mountain. The dancing lights of people's head torches slowly moving up made it almost firefly-like and magical. I was going well, I thought, after two hours in, but that was probably because I couldn't see what I was attacking.

It started to get lighter, and when we reached about a third of the way up, we took a very welcome break as we all sat in awe to watch the sunrise over this breathtakingly beautiful mountain. It was about 0500 hours, and everything, including our bodies, was instantly beginning to warm up with the emerging sunrise!

I could have sat there all day watching this scene. It was like when you're on a plane, above the clouds, and you can see the sun in the distance. Exactly like that!
I was star gazing and completely lost in the moment. For a brief moment I forgot where I was –but was quickly brought back to reality by a thundering "Let's go men," which broke the spell, and got my adrenaline pumping again.

Effortlessly, I snapped back into crazy mode and began walking again. It was only then that I looked up at our route, and began to see our daunting task unfolding before my eyes.

IT WAS HUGE – I mean like proper fucking huge!

The ground was like sand and it was at a sixty-degree angle. It was beautiful and nasty at the same time.

I had to take my arctic jacket off as I began to sweat profusely due to the climbing, which seemed to be one step forward and literally two steps back, for quite some time.

I cursed to myself, 'This is fucking horrible', as the volcanic ash was blowing in my face, and, as I breathed, I was eating the stuff because I was so close to the ground. We reached another resting point after 5-6 hours, but we were still some distance away from the summit. We were all beginning to get tired. You could see it on everyone's faces - their morale was pretty low!

I was struggling with headaches at this point, so much so I could barely see, but I knew if I said anything I would become another casualty being carried down the mountain, and the whole climb would be cancelled for certain. So, I kept quiet. I was beginning to feel dizzy and faint. It felt as though I had a fridge on my back. One step forward and THREE back now. I was sliding back all the time. It seemed like I wasn't getting anywhere. It was frustrating the life out of me; I was getting really pissed off and angry. But driving me on was this urge to make it to the top.

We had to start zigzagging across the mountain now - which to me just added shit loads of time -but it was the quickest and most efficient way to get up at this point. In my case though, it meant

that I was sliding down sideways now - and I got even more pissed off! "How long have we got, for fuck's sake, just tell me don't fucking lie" I kept saying!
I needed to calm down - so I sat there for ten minutes ranting to myself and the team were reassuring me; but it wasn't helping. It was just making me worse and more pissed off! They meant well, but it made me feel worse.

I calmed myself down, and I set off again. 'Just keep going for another hour' I mumbled to myself, 'then you can have another rest' but it was BRUTAL. I was literally taking ten minutes to walk 1 metre. The volcanic ash and this imaginary fridge kept dragging me down! My head

was getting tighter and my breathing was heavy! At this point, after 8-9 hours of climbing, I was only fuelled by a protein bar and some good old Kendal mint cake, which was giving me
heartburn!

Everything that could possibly go wrong was going wrong!

I had altitude sickness, headaches, blisters - I was tired and pissed off AND in my depressive state, I was really questioning life.

BUT I HAD TO KEEP GOING!!!

'Just keep your head down, James, and crack on'.

I didn't speak to anyone for a long time, I just wanted to try to get into a rhythm - but I couldn't! It was becoming too difficult - I was in pain, I was tired, I just wanted to give up and call it a day. This went on for about an hour. I was really questioning myself and my ability. All that was going through my head was 'Quit, quit, quit. Just stop and you can end this now and go down'.

I couldn't get these thoughts out of my head. It was horrible - so much so that I screamed and said "THAT'S IT! FUCK THIS!" I sat down, on the spot, and started to cry.

The tiredness, exhaustion and complete pain had finally got the better of me, I just couldn't go on anymore. I felt like a failure!

All I wanted to do was to be carried down the mountain. As I looked to my right I saw a stretcher and thought 'That looks so good - I could get carried down on that right now' but then I said to myself 'I would be in that dark hole with depression again if I did that'.

RIGHT! Get the fuck up and start climbing ! ! !

After 15 minutes of sulking, I got up and began to climb - 1-2-3-4 steps - and I wasn't any further on. I flung the towel in again and screamed as loud as I could! "

I CAN'T FUCKING DO THIS ANYMORE!"

I was in the hurt locker and I wasn't coming out! I needed to find something. I needed to dig deep into my resilience reserves. I needed to man up and go get up! I came here to complete this and I wasn't going to be defeated.

"ARRRGGGHHH!" I screamed.

One of the team came over and said quietly too me, "It's OK if you want to quit now.

You have done great". That made me want to get up even more! No way was I quitting, I needed words of encouragement, not demoralising shit like that!
I put my gloves back on and cracked on. This time there was no stopping me! Little did I know that I still had another 4 hours of this - but the summit was getting closer, which made me dig in even more. I began to filter all the negative thoughts out of my head and fill them

with positive ones, I found my second wind, or should I say my 10th. I was severely exhausted but somehow found the inner strength to just keep moving closer and closer one step at a time. Then BOOM!

We were confronted by a sheer rock face! Vertical with no way around it! I had to get up and over it!

To this day, I'm still not sure how I did it, but somehow I did get over those rocks. I was dizzy and not feeling good at all. I felt selfish for not telling anyone how I felt but

I came here to get up this mountain, and that was precisely what I was going to do!
We had been on the go for 13 solid hours at this point, when we were presented with this rock face. I was completely spent, but I knew, once I was over it, I would be back on good ground again, and that spurred me on.

Somehow, I got up and over it and felt a massive rush of adrenaline come over me!!!

I could see the guides stood at the summit all singing.
'
That's it. That's it, I have done it, keep going, keep going.'

I looked back down the mountain and it was engulfed in clouds rushing up the valley - the guides were singing to me as I reached the top! They picked me up and tossed me into the air. As they threw me up and down, I was crying tears of joy. Then I sat there with my head in my hands as I came to terms with what I had just achieved. I knew then that what I had done was monumental, but I just couldn't take it all in.

I was spent - my energy was totally depleted. I felt sick, tired, my blisters on my legs were screaming at me!

But now, we needed to get down.

I just wanted to get down!

One of the guides picked me up like a little child and put me on his back. "Let's go Simba" he said, as he literally started running down the mountain with me hanging on for dear life. The rock face that we had just struggled to climb blurred under his feet.

He just jumped down it as if it wasn't there, I just clung to him like a baby baboon to its mother. All I wanted was to get off this fucking mountain!

We had all been climbing it for 15 hours when this 'superhuman' guide put me on his back, running down the mountain!!! He took turns with another one of the guides, who, before we started the climb 15 hours ago, had already run up to the summit on his own, just to prove to us that he was fit enough to get us there!

These men were machines!!!

We got about a quarter of the way down in just 15 minutes when we spotted that stretcher that I had craved earlier. You know, the one I wanted to get on when I was going to quit. Well now it WAS my time to get on it!

I had climbed the mountain completely unaided and I couldn't give a shit exactly how I got down! I strapped myself into this makeshift stretcher and they began to pull me down. I put my hood up, my scarf over my face and I just lay there. I was in heaven.

I think they got me to base camp in about 45 minutes! They literally ran down the fucking mountain. I felt bad because I left the others to walk down - but it would have taken several hours to get back down if I'd walked, and I was completely done in!

As I was getting off the stretcher, I put my legs back on, then I turned round to look at what I had achieved.

KILIMANJARO, in all its glory.

It was hard to take it all in. What the fuck have I just done? How did I do that?
It slowly began to creep in. I had just climbed Kilimanjaro - completely unaided. . . I did what I set out to do. . . I was battered and tired, but now I was back to where we'd set off from 15 hours earlier.

I sat on my bed and started to take my legs off. I was damaged. Badly blistered. I took my rubber liners off and there must have been a pint of sweat and blood pouring out. I couldn't bear to take the blister tape off, everything was too sore, but it had to be done! I needed to treat the wounds. I got a quick – necessary - wash and sorted my admin out - clean clothes, and a hot drink! Just what I needed!

Just then the others came walking through the door – all, like me, absolutely spent.

We all sat there taking in what we had just achieved. It all felt surreal and I couldn't comprehend why we had done it. My mind was in a fog. I was soooo tired, I needed sleep, and also, now I had stopped working, I was freezing! So, I put my coat on and jumped in my doss bag.

I think I was awake for less than ten seconds before I was out like a light and snoring!!!

Aftermath
The morning after the day before that I'd climbed a massive mountain with no legs - I couldn't move! It felt as though I had been run over by a double-decker bus and then tackled by the whole England rugby team.

Was it all a dream?

I still couldn't believe what I had achieved! When you come to think of it it's pretty fucking epic that I had just completely pushed my own limits further than I thought possible, and proved that nothing is impossible. I'd just climbed the tallest free-standing mountain in the World.

I couldn't wait to call home and tell them the good news. The last time I had been in touch was 3 days ago, so it was so good to hear my wife's voice and break the news.

She couldn't believe it. . . I couldn't believe it!

I was already thinking about what I could do next. I wanted more of what I had just done - but I just didn't know what! I knew it was going to be something to do with mountains as I'd completely fallen in love with them on this trip. Even more so than I had done in the past! I had found my purpose in life - to climb mountains!!!

After nearly 10 years of battling demons, I had discovered a purpose to my life - I think I could justifiably now call myself a mountaineer.

I forget which famous philosopher once said that "All we need to make us completely happy is something to be enthusiastic about", but he was totally correct; and here's why - When you set yourself a goal which is as big as this, it completely takes your mind off the shit, negative, thoughts that rush around your head. This becomes your sole focus which keeps you on the right track; the planning, the fitness training, the meetings with the team; all play a big part in the overall journey, even before actually starting the climbing and hiking training, your life is entirely engulfed!

Don't get me wrong, whenever I am on a mountain there always comes a point when I literally question my entire existence and ask myself what the hell I am doing on yet another mountain; suffering the pain, the tiredness, and being totally pissed off! BUT that is all part of the process

towards becoming a stronger person - a stronger version of yourself. It gives you the belief that you can go even further than you ever thought possible; all totally beneficial and true! just 6 months before I summited Kilimanjaro I had never set foot on a mountain with no legs!

Previously it had taken me 3-4 hours to climb just 1km up a hill - 4 months later I had conquered

Helvellyn in the Lake District (in the winter!) and then 2 months after that I reached the summit of Kilimanjaro - all through believing in myself!!!

I completely winged it from start to finish and put the trust in my mindset and a little bit of fitness; but when you are tired and your body is completely depleted of energy, all you have left is your mindset - if that is strong, then you can achieve anything that you want to!

Peaks climbed
Kilimanjaro
Snowdon
Helvellyn
Old man of Coniston
Grisedale Pike
Pen y Fan
Pen y Ghent
Catbells
North Yorkshire Moors
.... (To Be Continued) ... ...

ACKNOWLEDGMENTS

The first person I want to acknowledge/thank is my wife Naiomi - I am not sure if that is correct word to use here!

I met Naiomi 1 month before I went to Afghanistan, ONE MONTH! I went over there and within 4 weeks I was a completely different person, well I was the same guy but just looked different with no legs. We spoke about everything when I was in hospital but she never saw an issue, she still saw me as the James who went to war, I was still the same person to her. Naiomi was studying at uni in Liverpool and for her to completely drop everything and visit me every single day while in her last year is something that I can never repay. She has been my rock through all
of this. We got engaged in 2010, I proposed over some fish and chips. I knew I wanted to spend the rest of my life with her. We married in 2018 at the Le Petit Chateau in Northumberland.

If it weren't for my wife, I would most probably be dead! She continues to push me even though

I drive her mad at times, but we are stronger than ever and our life has only just begun!

I want to say a special mention to my son Jake who is turning into a great young man

My Mam (Denise) and Les, who are always there no matter what, even though I put her through hell! What son doesn't haha.

My Brother & Sister, Nathan & Caroline

The In laws Kay, Chris and Brian

A special mention to my mates who have pushed me through the shit times and never let me down! No names mentioned you know who you are! I love you's all.

A special mention to my childhood friend, best man and all-round good guy, Ben Grainger. I want to share this little story which completely gave me a different outlook on life when I was first injured."During a night out on the piss I started to become unwell, at this point in time I had a colostomy bag attached to me. I went to the toilet to change it and, as I looked down, I had seen the bag had burst all over my white shirt (brown now). I sat there in my wheelchair and began to feel sorry for myself, getting upset and angry about the whole situation. I was only out of hospital about 6 months at this point so the feelings were still raw. Ben came into the toilet, started shouting me. I was there sobbing like a baby ashamed, embarrassed and just a complete mess. Ben comes over and asks what's up. I showed him, he said that's fine mate we will get you cleaned up and we will go get tanked up at the bar! All I wanted to do was go home and end my life but instead Ben booked a

taxi, we went to my mam's house, he put me in the bath, got me a clean shirt, poured me a quick drink and booked a taxi back to the club where we had just had all this drama. If it wasn't for that moment then I don't think I would have ever recovered, it changed
my outlook to life and taught me that no matter what you can always come out the other end smiling. We ended up staying out that night till about 0300, after that we went home, sat on my mam's living room floor and drank neat vodka while watching Taken, the Movie!!

John Gilpin and Roy Glendening who were my welfare officers at the time of my injury. John went and broke the news to my family, now we remain good friends and we help each other, we get out hiking in the Lake District, in the mountains, which is great for our mental health.

A very special mention to my team in Afghanistan who saved my life, "**The Men**".
2 York's OMLT - Amber 58 "stay frosty"
James Frost
John Wright
John Hardman
Rob Mac
Dom Taylor
Michael Oldroyd
Gordan Metcalf
Willo
Craig Bailey

The truth is I could spend all day writing here on who has helped me and pushed me forward. I want to thank everyone collectively who is/has been in my life during my bad times and during my good times and continue to be there, without all of you I wouldn't be the person I am today, thank you.

Thank you ALL.

Printed in Great Britain
by Amazon